Language in Multicultural Classrooms

Viv Edwards

Batsford Academic and Educational Ltd
London

for Chris, Dafydd, Ceri and Siân

© Viv Edwards 1983
First published 1983

Typeset by Progress Filmsetting Limited
and printed in Great Britain by
Billings Ltd
Worcester.
for the publishers
Batsford Academic and Educational Ltd
4 Fitzhardinge Street, London W1H 0AH

British Library Cataloguing in Publication
Data

Edwards, Viv
Language in multicultural classrooms—
(Education in multicultural society)
1. Children of minorities—Education—Great Britain
2. Language arts—Great Britain
I. Title   II. Series
372.6   LC3747.G7
ISBN 0 7134 45084

Contents

Acknowledgments

This book has been written during a period of great professional uncertainty for myself and countless other researchers. Educational cutbacks at all levels have meant that many of us have never known the security of a permanent job and are currently faced with either unemployment or the daunting prospect of proceeding from one temporary post to the next. The difficulties of persevering in a professional and financial vacuum such as this, especially when long term prospects remain bleak, need hardly be spelt out in further detail.

The economic hardship of this situation has, in my case, been cushioned by the fact that I am a married woman whose husband is in employment. However, being a married woman and, in particular, a mother, raises other problems. On the one hand, our intellectual needs and the possible contribution we can make in our field are often trivialized or overlooked. On the other hand, we are expected to perform on a par with male colleagues without any understanding of the immense physical and emotional demands which society places upon us. The one commodity which most working mothers crave is a wife! I have the next best thing: a husband who understands my professional aspirations and provides all the practical support which a full-time job allows; and parents who are similarly supportive. Acknowledgments of help provided during the course of writing this book must, therefore, go primarily to Chris Morriss, Hett Edwards and Tom Edwards.

This is not, of course, to minimize the help I have received from colleagues. Jenny Cheshire, Steve Hoyle, Alex McLeod, Cliff Moon, Bridie Raban, John Richmond, Joanna Studdert and Sylvaine Wiles have all read and made extremely helpful comments on drafts of various chapters. I would also like to acknowledge the help I have received from students at Bulmershe College of Higher Education, particularly those on the First School Language course. I have taught this course jointly with Heather Lyons and Judy Keiner who have allowed me to develop my own ideas and have also given freely of their own experience. Thanks, too, are due to staff and pupils of Redlands Primary School, Reading, who have provided me with much valuable observation and material, and to the many Berkshire and Buckinghamshire teachers who have helped me to formulate and try out new ideas. I would like to single out, in particular, Audrey Gregory, Angela Redfern and Robin Richardson, the adviser for multicultural education for Berkshire. Finally, thanks are due to my children and their friends who have allowed me, albeit inadvertently, to observe the resources of children's language both outside and inside the classroom; and to Abigail Gillett, for her interested and intelligent approach to typing the manuscript.

I should also like to thank those authors and publishers who have kindly given permission for the reproduction in the text of copyright material, as follows: Harold Rosen and Tony Burgess for the table on p. 20 reprinted from *Languages and Dialects of London School Children*, Ward Lock Educational, 1980; Jim Cummins for the chart on p.36 from 'Biliteracy, Language Proficiency and Educational Programs', in *The Social Psychology of Reading*, edited by John Edwards, Silver Spring, Maryland: Institute of Modern Languages, 1981; John Wright for permission to quote from *Bilingualism in Education*, Issues in Race and Education, 1982; D. G. Halliday for permission to reproduce part of the paper submitted as evidence to the Committee of Enquiry into the Education of Children from Ethnic Minority Groups by participants at the DES conference on Mother Tongue Teaching at Bedford College of Higher Education, September, 1981; Michael Stubbs for the dialogue reproduced on p.81-2 from *Language, Schools and Classrooms*, Methuen, 1976; Edward Arnold (publisher) for the dialogue on p.88 recorded by children in Donna Anaman's class at the Princess May Junior School and originally used in 'Language Issues in the Multicultural Classroom', from *Language in School and Community*, edited by Neil Mercer; Cliff Moon and Bridie Raban for the chart on p.99 adapted from *A Question of Reading*, Macmillan, 1980; Schools Council Publications for the chart on p.98 taken from *Extending Beginning Reading* by V. Southgate, H. Arnold and S. Johnson, Heinemann Educational Books, 1981; Joanna Studdert and Sylvaine Wiles for permission to quote from 'Children's Writing in the Multilingual Classroom', Occasional Paper, Spring, 1982, Centre for Urban Educational Studies; and Frank Smith for permission to quote from *Writing and the Writer*, Heinemann Educational Books, 1982.

Viv Edwards
Reading, October 1982

Editor's Preface

It is now coming to be more widely recognized that Britain is a culturally diverse society, and has been for centuries. Variations of belief and behaviour according to region, religion, class and ethnicity have always existed, but we are now increasingly conscious of the greater potential for enrichment – as well as for conflict – that these variations make possible. This new series will seek to explore some of the more salient educational issues presented by cultural diversity, and with particular reference to *ethnicity*. It will aim to contribute to the skills and understanding of teachers, teacher training, educational administrators and policy-makers, whose concern is to provide for the educational needs of all children growing up in a multicultural society.

Language in Multicultural Classrooms has been contributed by Dr Viv Edwards, a well-known expert in the field, who offers a comprehensive but yet immensely readable review of both the practical and theoretical issues relating to linguistic diversity in modern Britain. Those who teach, and those who train or employ teachers will readily recognize the classroom situations which Dr Edwards describes, and will find her careful analysis, enlivened as it is by examples of children's speech and writing, helpful and enlightening.

Maurice Craft
University of Nottingham

1 Language as a classroom issue

Introduction

The central argument put forward in this book is that the linguistic diversity to be found in British schools rarely constitutes an educational problem, but that attitudes towards this diversity are of critical importance. Language and identity are so strongly intermeshed that any attack on the way we speak is likely to be perceived as an attack on our values and integrity. Thus, if children's language is undervalued or rejected in school, they may well respond by withdrawal or defiance. By the same token, recognition of their language gives teachers the opportunity to show pupils that they are valued and accepted. This surely constitutes a more promising starting point for motivating children to learn than constant criticism and rejection.

The idea that the school should acknowledge the language of the home is by no means new and has emerged as a debating point from time to time in educational circles for almost a hundred years (Hollingworth, 1977). Nevertheless, it remains a controversial issue, primarily because of the importance attached in our society to standard English. For many years, it was assumed that English speakers and, in particular, standard English speakers have access to an intrinsically superior language and some people still behave as if this were the case. A rapid survey of the relevant literature (see, for example, Newbolt, 1921; Spens, 1939; Fagan, 1958; Weightman, 1982) can certainly leave the impression that the standard speaker has a monopoly of precision, expressiveness and understanding. Yet such a position is based on appeals to emotion rather than reasoned argument.

It is only in relatively recent times that we have moved from a prescriptive to a descriptive view of language. An important realisation which has accompanied this change in emphasis is that all languages and dialects are equally adequate, well-formed and rule-governed: there is no evidence that one variety is inherently superior to another and qualities such as logic or precision can be more properly attributed to individual speakers than to the language which they happen to speak. This position is not based on sentimentality or wishful thinking, but on careful analysis and observation of speech in a wide range of situations (see, for instance, Labov, 1966; 1969; Trudgill, 1974; Milroy, 1980; Cheshire, 1982b).

Language attitudes and social prediction

Unfortunately linguistic equality does not extend to social equality and some languages and dialects are distinctly more equal than others. It is not difficult to understand why this should be the case. Our speech provides listeners with as rich a diversity of information as the clothes we wear or the surroundings in which we live. It can reveal the country or region we come from, our racial origin and our social class background. But in addition to this factual information, speech can have a predictive or diagnostic function. A vast body of research evidence shows that members of subordinate groups in society - those who belong to lower socio-economic classes, ethnic or racial minorities or women - are evaluated less favourably in terms of competence and status than members of the dominant group (cf. Giles & Powesland, 1975; Ryan & Giles, 1982). It should be noted, however, that whereas the first kind of inference from speech is based on fact, the second draws on our stereotypes and expectations and is not necessarily objectively true.

This can be illustrated by an exercise which I sometimes undertake when starting to work with a new group of students or teachers. I ask a number of questions about myself: Where do I come from? What social class do my parents belong to? What kind of school did I go to? What do I vote in an election? Are my allegiances to my cultural background weak or strong? The interesting thing to emerge from this exercise is not whether the answers given are right or wrong (quite often they are wrong), but the high degree of consensus which emerges in the group.

It is equally noteworthy that the status and competence attached to standard English, particularly when spoken with 'Received Pronunciation' or a BBC accent, is recognised by all speakers in Britain, whether or not they are standard speakers themselves. Such attitudes are shared by adults and children alike. It has been demonstrated, for instance, that children between the ages of 4 and 6 make judgements about differences in speech style which are remarkably similar to those made by adult speakers in their communities (Day, 1982). At first glance, this would seem to make the school's task of teaching standard English an easy one. Since the acquisition of the standard marks the route to educational success and social mobility, and since all speakers recognise the prestige of the standard, it is perhaps surprising that we are not automatically a nation of standard English speakers. There is, however, another vitally important dimension in attitudes towards language, for while dialect speaking and bilingual children share the dominant group's perceptions of standard English as the marker of status and power, they also have strong feelings about the value of their own speech which they associate with solidarity, integrity, social attractiveness and persuasive quality (Ryan & Giles, 1982). The strength of these attributes is such that many speakers are not prepared to compromise their own sense of group identity by abandoning dialect or foreign-accented speech in favour of standard English.

Teacher attitudes towards language

Teachers are first and foremost people and can therefore be expected to respond to speech cues in the same way as the rest of the population. However, schools provide an extremely important point of contact between speakers of different languages and dialects, where considerable significance is attached to the acquisition of standard English. The present focus on teacher attitudes towards language is thus a reflection of the importance of their position rather than an attempt to portray them as a group any more or less prone to stereotyping behaviour.

It has been suggested that attitudes towards language are more critical in an educational setting than actual linguistic differences. Research on teacher attitudes certainly lends support to this position. A number of studies confirm that speech style is important in teacher evaluation and point to an unmistakable bias in favour of middle class pupils. Frender, Brown & Lambert (1970), for instance, found that those lower-class pupils who were doing well in school had a distinctly different speech style from those who were under-achieving. Seligman, Tucker & Lambert (1972) used combinations of good drawings and compositions with poor or good voices, based on previous evaluations of student teacher judges. These were presented to a new set of student teacher judges who considered voice when judging intelligence and both voice and physical appearance in judging capability. J. Edwards (1977; 1979a) also provides evidence which suggests that teachers react to a stereotype of the 'disadvantaged' pupil. In his work with teacher and student teacher evaluations of primary school children in Dublin, working class children were consistently viewed less favourably than their middle class peers.

Still further studies demonstrate an ethnic or racial dimension to teacher evaluations. Granger, Matthews, Quay & Verner (1977) show that teacher ratings of black and white children in the United States display both social class and racial bias. Williams et al.'s (1976) work with white, black and Mexican American children confirms this tendency. V. Edwards (1979) shows how a hierarchy of preferences emerges in a British setting, whereby middle class children are evaluated most favourably, then working class children and finally West Indian children. These findings are all the more striking in view of the fact that the same child was evaluated more positively when she spoke with a working class English accent than when she used a West Indian dialect.

There is strong evidence that the teachers who took part in these various research projects were reacting to how the children spoke rather than what they said. Williams et al. (op. cit.), for example, isolated two potentially independent dimensions for evaluation: confidence/eagerness and standardness/non-standardness of speech. It is highly significant that teachers consistently rated children across the two dimensions, rather than favourably on one dimension and unfavourably on the other. Moreover, they are frequently prepared to offer further information which is indicative of stereotyping behaviour. Choy & Dodd (1976), for instance, show that teachers were ready to make judgements not only about children's confidence and classroom behaviour, but also on how happy their marriages were likely to be. V. Edwards (op. cit.) found that student teachers were willing to state whether or not a child would be a valuable member of the class on the basis of a 30 second extract in which they talked about a visit to the dentist.

The exploration of the relationship between teacher expectation and pupil performance has been fraught with difficulty (cf. Thorndike, 1968; Snow, 1969). None the less a good deal of evidence exists which suggests that teacher attitudes towards individual pupils may play an important role in their academic achievement (see Pidgeon, 1970, and Verma & Bagley, 1975, for reviews of the research evidence in this area). All of the studies reported above were conducted in highly artificial experimental conditions and it does not necessarily follow that the stereotyped views expressed under such conditions will be translated into differing patterns of teacher response to children in the classroom. However, we should, at the very least, be alert to the ways in which speech cues trigger social stereotypes and to the danger that these stereotypes will be translated into reality in the school.

It ain't bad grammar, it's just dialect

In view of the vital role which language plays in social behaviour of all kinds, it is hardly surprising that it has emerged as a central issue in education. Yet all too often the importance of language is exaggerated: school success or failure is explained in terms of actual linguistic differences between children rather than society's attitudes towards those differences. It is important to remember that the points of similarity in the acquisition and development of language, both within and across cultures, are far more striking than individual or inter-group differences. Under normal circumstances all children learn not only to recognize and replicate the linguistic patterns of those around them but also when it is appropriate to speak in a particular way. The ability of children to learn another language or dialect depends both on exposure to the new variety and on their motivation to identify with people who use it. The differences between most British dialects and standard English, for instance, are relatively small and should not constitute a major learning problem. The failure of many dialect speaking children to acquire standard English must therefore reflect feelings of alienation and discomfort which can only be compounded by teachers who covertly or openly express the view that non-standard speech is unacceptable.

This is a position which will be familiar to any reader with a background in sociolinguistics or the social psychology of language. It is, however, by no means universally accepted. A report of a serious discussion by Cheshire (1982a) of linguistic conflict in education was cynically headlined in *The Sunday Times* of 18 April, 1982 as, 'It ain't bad grammar, it's just dialect' and provoked an angry correspondence. Suggestions by Sutcliffe and Richmond in Sutcliffe (1982) that British Black English has an important part to play in the education of black children have met with equally hostile reactions. Weightman (1982), for example, makes his position very clear:

> While Standard English-speakers should recognize the validity of black English within its cultural context, it is not their function, especially if they are teachers, to encourage blacks in the creation of a ghetto mentality.

Interestingly, such negative comments come from both ends of the political spectrum. There is anxiety in certain radical quarters, for instance, that many aspects of 'multicultural education' are designed to contain dissent and distract attention from the legitimate social and political grievances of oppressed groups. Thus, on the cover of Stone's *The Education of the Black Child in Britain,* we find:

In many schools steel band sessions and West Indian dialect classes replace basic skills, and among teachers 'relating to kids' was valued above sheer teaching ability.

It must be recognized that comments such as this are a useful reminder of potential dangers in attempting to acknowledge linguistic and cultural diversity in our schools. It should be stressed, however, that these dangers are potential rather than inevitable. All too often those who present arguments against building on linguistic diversity in the classroom, both from the traditional right and left, give rise to a completely unnecessary polarization. They demonstrate a total misunderstanding of the position espoused by Cheshire, Richmond, Sutcliffe, Trudgill and many other writers who are in fact arguing that the use of dialect should complement standard English and not that dialect should replace it. Their aim is not to deny children access to standard English but to point to ways in which teachers ignore at their peril the important links between language and identity and the counterproductive nature of efforts to impose the standard.

Misunderstandings of this kind are met by linguists with a mixture of incredulity and frustration (cf. Trudgill, 1979a). Arguments regarding the linguistic adequacy of all languages and dialects have been carefully assembled and frequently aired in the literature, yet the continuing prejudice of non-linguists makes it necessary to restate these arguments even to the point of tedium. The fact that standard English is not intrinsically superior to other languages and dialects will therefore form a recurrent theme in this book, as will the implications of this position.

Linguistic minorities in British schools

Although linguistic diversity is not a new discussion point in educational circles, for many years attention was firmly focused on the position of British dialect speakers. However, the arrival throughout the 1960s and early 1970s of non-English speaking children and speakers of overseas dialects of English has had the effect of both stimulating the debate on language in education and helping it to develop in a new direction. There has been a growing appreciation of the skills which bilingual children bring with them to school and the value of building upon these skills rather than ignoring them. The important part which language plays in children's sense of identity is also receiving increased recognition and there is a strong feeling in many quarters that a positive self-concept is a prerequisite for successful learning. Issues such as identity, respect and building on existing skills are easy to recognize in the case of children from very different linguistic backgrounds. They have also served to highlight many needs which have been long overlooked in indigenous British children. It would be illogical for teachers who accept the importance of recognizing linguistic diversity for bilingual pupils to fail to apply the same principles to children who speak non-standard dialects of English, since the issues are the same.

The presence of ethnic minority children in British schools has thus stimulated considerable discussion of the need to reflect the multicultural composition of present day society in various aspects of the curriculum, including language (cf. Little & Willey, 1981; Jeffcoate, 1979). It is vitally important to stress that the understanding of 'multicultural' in this book applies not only to bilingual children, but to speakers of non-standard dialects of English which have originated both in Britain and overseas. The potential audience is thus not simply teachers in inner city schools, but those working with dialect speaking children all over the United Kingdom. Since standard English is spoken only by a small minority of British people, it seems reasonable to assume that the issues raised will be of relevance to the majority of teachers.

What about the parents?

Parents may find recent developments in the direction of 'hospitality to diversity' (cf. Levine, 1982) strange and bewildering. They recognize the status of English, particularly standard English, and may be puzzled by changes in policy on language. Some parents, especially those of West Indian origin, may be extremely hostile to change, perceiving it as yet another attempt to deny their children equality of opportunity. It is important to remember, however, that there have been many areas of change in British schools. The introduction of sex education, for instance, has given rise to considerable controversy. Likewise, many parents have been completely befuddled by radical changes in the teaching of maths and reading. Parents are seldom if ever directly involved in the formulation of new policy and teachers justify change on the grounds that, in their professional judgement, given curriculum innovations will be of educational benefit to the children. There is, however, a growing feeling of the need for accountability - witness the Schools Information Act 1982 - and it is certainly a matter of common sense that new developments are more likely to succeed if the underlying rationale is clearly explained.

Most parents' fears on language matters will be allayed by the reassurance that linguistic diversity is being used as a classroom resource which complements rather than replaces the use of standard English. The chapters which follow contain numerous examples of children who have shown greater interest and application in reading and writing by being directed to literature and themes which draw on languages and dialects other than the standard. Success breeds success and the educational benefits of this approach should be clearly spelt out.

The signs are that parents will respond enthusiastically. The introduction of mother tongue classes within a school, for instance, is usually marked by parents who have previously had little or no contact with the school adopting a far more open attitude and even volunteering their help. English speaking parents also tend to react with interest when other languages and dialects are introduced into aspects of their children's work, particularly when they are informed of the underlying rationale. Some parents, of course, will remain sceptical. The responsibility of the school, however, lies simply in explaining how and why a given course of action is being pursued. Parents' feelings must obviously be taken into account, but policy decisions should be based on educational benefits rather than linguistic prejudice.

The importance of a school language policy

The case for adopting more liberal attitudes towards language than has been the rule in British education is based on both practical and philosophical considerations. On the one hand, by creating an atmosphere in which linguistic diversity is regarded as a classroom resource rather than an educational problem, children are more likely to feel a valued part of the school and better motivated to learn. On the other hand, devaluation of children's language shows a lack of respect for them and the community to which they belong and is likely to produce a strong reaction against the language and values of the school. Many individual teachers have great sympathy with these arguments and adapt the content of the curriculum and their teaching methods accordingly. Unless a school language policy is formulated, however, the messages which children receive will be confusing and contradictory.

The importance of school language policies was clearly outlined in the Bullock Report, *A Language for Life*. Yet the main emphasis in this document, and most other discussions of language policy, is on 'language across the curriculum' and the notion that language should be the concern of all teachers and not simply the English specialist (see Chapter 5). The recognition of the importance of children's own language in learning and the ways in which academic language can hinder rather than help this process is extremely important. Guidance on matters relating to linguistic diversity, however, is contained in general statements rather than specific advice.

The chapters which follow attempt to remedy this weakness by outlining a number of issues which are of immediate relevance to teachers in multicultural classrooms: How can I go about creating an atmosphere which is supportive of linguistic diversity? Do I write down a child's dictation word for word or do I 'translate' it into standard English? How do I respond when children replace a word in a reading passage with one from their own langauge or a second language learning error? Should I correct dialect forms and second language learning errors in children's writing? How can I distinguish between features of the child's own linguistic system and genuine mistakes? Are some approaches to dialect and second language material likely to be perceived as patronizing or threatening by children? Can this be avoided? It is vitally important that schools should adopt a joint policy on questions such as these, based on informed discussion, rather than approach the subject in an *ad hoc* and haphazard way.

An overview of the book

The book falls into two main parts. First it is hoped to provide an historical background to the various language issues which confront teachers in multicultural classrooms. Attitudes to language and approaches to language teaching have not evolved in a social and political vacuum and, in order to understand current thought, it is important to trace the development of language policies and practices in British schools. The next four chapters will consider the dimensions of linguistic diversity, focusing first on bilingual children (and drawing on discussion of both English teaching and the 'Mother Tongue' issue); then on speakers of British Black English; and finally on speakers of regional non-standard dialects of English.

The second part of the book looks at three vital areas of the curriculum - talk, reading and writing. It attempts to present an overview of theoretical issues in each of these areas and their relevance for children from different linguistic backgrounds, as well as outlining helpful practical strategies which are consistent with the theoretical positions outlined. Finally the reader is offered suggestions for further reading, details of materials referred to in the text and useful addresses.

2 Bilingualism and the teaching of English as a second language

The extent of linguistic diversity
In most parts of the world multilingualism is an accepted fact of life rather than a rarity. Something in the region of 300 languages and many more dialects belonging to three separate families of languages are spoken in the Indian sub-continent. A little nearer home, at least 14 different languages are spoken natively in Roumania by various sections of the population. In comparison, the linguistic composition of Britain seems remarkably homogeneous. Certainly this is the underlying premise on which school language policy has been based and until very recently the only acceptable language in the classroom has been standard English.

Yet the notion of linguistic homogeneity can be shown to be a total myth, both today and in the past. There have always been sizeable, though declining, numbers of Welsh and Gaelic speakers, and large Irish and Jewish populations can be traced back to the last century (cf. Rosen & Burgess, 1980). Italian and Cypriot communities have grown considerably since the last war, but more recent arrivals were in fact joining family and friends who had been settled in Britain well before 1939. Polish, Ukrainian, Hungarian and other refugees, expelled or in voluntary exile, have also swelled the ranks of ethnic minorities in Britain. However, the biggest wave of immigration came in direct response to the industrial expansion and boom economy of the 1950s. The largest numbers of newcomers came from India, Pakistan, East Africa, the West Indies and, to a much lesser extent, Hong Kong. This influx of New Commonwealth immigrants began in the mid-1950s and continued until successively restrictive legislation brought immigration to a virtual halt in the late 1960s (Hiro, 1973). More recently, political events such as the expulsion of Ugandan Asians and the flight of the Vietnamese Boat People have swelled existing minorities and created new ones. The linguistic heritage of this population movement is certainly not consistent with the notion of a monolingual, monocultural Britain.

The precise size of these groups is extremely difficult to estimate.

The main problem is that official census and Department of Education and Science (DES) statistics are based on country of origin, rather than the language spoken, and the one is not always an accurate indicator of the other. It does not necessarily follow, for instance, that someone born in Germany or Poland speaks German or Polish, since migrants from both countries include significant minorities whose *lingua franca* is Yiddish. East African Asians may speak Punjabi, Gujarati or Hindi. Hong Kong Chinese are likely to speak Cantonese or Hakka. Yet country of origin represents one of the few available sources of information on minority populations and can at least give some indication as to the numbers and distribution of linguistic minority groups. Campbell-Platt (1976), for instance, estimates on the basis of 1971 census figures that linguistic minorities in Britain include, in roughly descending order of numerical importance, speakers of Punjabi, Urdu, Bengali, Gujarati, German, Polish, Italian, Greek, Spanish and Cantonese or Hakka.

The need for more accurate information on the linguistic composition of ethnic minorities has recently been recognized by two teams of researchers who have attempted to go beyond indirect statistical evidence on country of origin. The first team consisted of Harold Rosen, Tony Burgess and teacher researchers in London schools; the second team made up the Linguistic Minorities Project (LMP) directed by Verity Saifullah Khan. Both groups were based at the London University Institute of Education.

The pioneering efforts in this area were made by Harold Rosen and Tony Burgess. In a short term study of linguistic diversity funded by the DES, information was collected from 4,600 first year pupils in 28 London secondary schools. Questionnaires were completed by teachers who drew on their own existing knowledge and talk with pupils, usually in small groups. Analysis of the data showed that 6 per cent of the children spoke some 55 named world languages between them (see Table 1). This study also indicates differing patterns of bilingualism, giving information, for example, on which languages are dominant and whether children are literate in their mother tongue.

Most of our information understandably centres on London, the cosmopolitan home of about half the linguistic minority populations of Britain. It is none the less important to build up a picture of linguistic diversity in other parts of the country and the initiatives of the Linguistic Minorities Project (1983) are very welcome in this respect. The project has set out to establish the range of diversity in all schools in a small number of LEAs, which include Bradford, Coventry, Cambridgeshire and Haringey, and to study the perceptions and language use of pupils in a sample of secondary

Table 1: Languages other than English, where spoken by one or more pupils

European	African	South Asian	Mid-Eastern	Far Eastern	Other
Greek	Yoruba	Gujarati	Iranian	Cantonese	French
Turkish	Hausa	Bengali	'Moroccan'	Chinese (new)	Creoles
Italian	Ibo	Punjabi	Arabic	standard	(Dominican,
Spanish	'Gambian'	Hindi		Mandarin	St Lucian
German	Gur	Urdu		Japanese	Guyanese
Portuguese	Swahili	Katchi		Malay	Mauritian)
French	Twi	Nepalese			Maori
Dutch	Zulu	Pushtu			Maltese
Finnish	Afrikaans	Sinhalese			Romany
Gaelic		Tamil			
Hungarian					
Polish					
Swedish					
Serbo-Croat					
Slovene					
Russian					
Armenian					
Latvian					
Yiddish					
Hebrew					
21	9	10	3	5	7

Total number of languages: 55

Source: Rosen and Burgess (1980) p. 63

schools in these authorities. The results of these surveys will be met with considerable interest when they are published in 1984.

The school response to bilingualism

The educational establishment has been extremely slow in perceiving and responding to the needs of its bilingual pupils. Inasmuch as a language policy existed in Britain during the first half of the twentieth century it focused on the unacceptability of Celtic languages and non-standard dialects of English in education and the importance of teaching the standard. British schools were monolingual, mono-cultural institutions, one of whose functions was to enlighten those who departed from received linguistic and cultural norms. The important population changes of the last three decades have thus given rise to serious challenges to accepted values and practices.

Immigration to and settlement in Britain in the mid- and late 1950s was an almost exclusively adult affair. It was not until the 1960s that heads of families were sufficiently settled to consider starting to send for dependents who had been left behind in the care of relatives. Housing shortgages ensured that the only supply of low-price accommodation was in decaying inner city areas where schools were often under-staffed and insufficiently resourced (cf. Newsom, 1963; Plowden, 1976). The arrival, throughout the school year, of considerable numbers of children of all ages, many of whom did not speak English, placed acute strain on teachers who were already working under difficult circumstances.

By the early 1960s it had become clear that the attitude of laissez-faire, frequently expressed in the comment 'They'll pick up English in the playground', was untenable. The first official advice came in the Ministry of Education pamphlet *English for Immigrants* which advocated the bringing together of non-English speaking children in one school for English classes and stressed the need for a 'carefully planned, intensive course making full use of modern methods of language teaching'. Such a recommendation depended, of course, on the availability of teachers of English as a Second Language. There were, however, few trained teachers in this field and no attempt was made to attract those working abroad to return or, until the late sixties, to train new teachers. Even today there is a shortage of specialist staff (Bakhsh & Walker, 1980; CRE, 1980).

Throughout this period, one of the main obstacles to the development of a coherent national language policy was the marked degree of local autonomy in the education systems of England and Wales. In the absence of advice from central government, each LEA evolved its own system for meeting immediate needs. Little information was available on developments in other schools and authorities and the overall result was, in the words of one government report, 'haphazard' (HMSO, 1973). The extent of diversity in provision is clearly illustrated by an extract from the 1973 report of the Parliamentary Select Committee on Race Relations and Immigration:

> Bristol has a large centre for secondary pupils and peripatetic teachers for primary ones; Haringey has no reception centre and no peripatetic teachers, but withdraws pupils within their own schools, with the backing of a resource centre, and, because of lack of space in schools, teaches some of them at home; Brent has a language centre for junior and secondary pupils, language classes at one high school and peripatetic teachers in infant schools; Ealing has immigrant reception classes in infant, junior and secondary schools and further withdrawal classes in a language centre for infants; Leicester has withdrawal classes in schools and no peripatetic teachers, but is thinking of setting up a reception centre;

Liverpool appears to do little but has a small language centre in one school and intends to set up a language development centre; Bolton has a language centre to which primary pupils are withdrawn for half a day each day, peripatetic teachers in primary schools and a sophisticated system of help in secondary schools (Select Committee on Race Relations and Immigration, Session 1972-3, Education: p.11).

Dispersal policies

During the early 1960s discussion was marked by a pre-occupation among public and politicians alike with the disruption to the normal class routine which could be posed by the presence of non-English speaking pupils. There was a similar concern about the concentration within any one school or class. At the election of March 1966 it became clear that opposition to immigration was not the vote catching issue that some had feared, but nevertheless, official policy at this time 'gave the accurate impression of having been devised under the pressure of circumstances and based on received ideas' (Rose et al., 1969: 289).

The first public protest about the presence of immigrant children in schools was staged by parents at two primary schools in Southall in 1963. Sir Edward Boyle, as Minister of Education, attended a meeting organized by the parents. Although he totally rejected the idea of separate education for immigrant children, he later referred in Parliament to one school which had become 'irretrievably immigrant' and, in order to prevent this happening elsewhere, suggested that LEAs should introduce zoning schemes which would limit the proportion of immigrant children within any one school to about 30 per cent (Hansard, Vol. 685, cols 433-444).

The Second Report of the Commonwealth Immigrants Advisory Committee (CIAC, 1964), a body set up by the Conservative government, was published the following year, but had been drafted at the time of the Southall troubles. Significantly, it stressed 'the dangers of the creation of immigrant schools' and suggested the possibility of 'arrangements to send children to some alternative school in order to preserve a reasonable balance'. The official policy was first set out, however, in the White Paper of 1965, *Immigration from the Commonwealth*, and the Department of Education and Science (DES) Circular 7/65 which was incorporated in summary form in part iii of the White Paper. The need for dispersal in areas of high immigrant population was a keynote of these documents:

> In order to maintain the standards of education in schools attended by large numbers of immigrant children with language difficulties, special arrangements must be made to teach them English... Such arrangements

can more easily be made, and the integration of the immigrants more easily achieved, if the proportion of immigrant children in a school is not allowed to rise too high (HMSO, 1965, paras 41-2)

In accordance with Circular 7/65, the maximum proportion of immigrant children normally acceptable in a school was felt to be 'about one third'. This attempt at formulation of policy was, however, beset with difficulties. No statistics were available in 1965 for either the number of immigrant children in schools, or the proportion of those children experiencing language difficulties. Equally worrying, it has never been made clear whether the dispersal policy was to apply to all immigrant children or only to those who could not speak English. In the final analysis, government worries appear to have been completely unfounded. The publication of an Inner London Education Authority (ILEA) report in 1967 on 52 primary schools where immigrant children formed more than one third of the pupils showed that non-immigrants in these schools achieved the same as the average for all pupils in ILEA schools on tests of English, Verbal Reasoning and Mathematics. The formulation of the dispersal policy also represented a basic contradiction of earlier policy, since the 1963 pamphlet, *English for Immigrants,* had stated quite clearly that the most satisfactory arrangement for the teaching of English involved bringing children together for classes in one school.

Local reaction to the dispersal scheme varied a great deal (cf. Rose et al., op.cit.: 272-3). Some LEAs were already operating their own schemes; others found the practical difficulties of implementing dispersal too great; still others rejected the notion, either on the grounds that it violated the principle of neighbourhood school, or because it could be perceived as discriminatory. The Plowden Report which appeared in 1967 also expressed strong reservations about dispersal and stressed that the only criteria for moving children to other schools should be language and other difficulties, and not simply their ethnic background. Yet, whatever the weakness of the policy which Power (1967: 6) described as 'one of the unexplained administrative curiosities of the decade', the White Paper did stimulate discussion and formulation of more constructive policies.

Language policy post-1965

Undoubtedly one of the most important influences on the formulation of policy in the post-1965 period was the work undertaken by June Derrick and her colleagues as part of 'The Leeds Project' (Derrick, 1967). Following proposals put forward by Derrick, the Schools Council, a government funded body, agreed to sponsor a feasibility study on LEA and classroom practices. On the basis of this study a three year project was commissioned and set up at the University of Leeds Institute of Education from September 1966. The Leeds Project aimed to develop an introductory two-term course in English as a Second language for children aged 8-13 years, a more advanced course for the same age group, and a course for newly arrived teenagers, as well as continuing research into the possibilities for 5-7 year olds. The extremely practical nature of the Project gave rise to a set of policy imperatives quite different from those which had informed the pre-1965 dispersal schemes. It showed that the most urgent need was for books and materials; that initial teacher training should be extended to include language teaching for immigrants and that in-service training in this area should also be provided; and that nursery schools should be set up in areas of immigrant settlement. The teaching of English as a second language emerged as a priority irrespective of the proportion of immigrants in a school, since these children would be unable either to participate fully in school life or compete on equal terms for jobs without an adequate command of English. The Project also served a useful teacher training fuction since approximately 150 teachers in 38 LEAs were involved in the trial of materials.

Another policy imperative which emerged in the wake of the 1965 White Paper was the need to collect accurate information on the distribution and language teaching needs of immigrant children. The collection of statistics in the early years of immigration had been avoided on the grounds that this action might be perceived as being discriminatory. It was not until January 1966 that Form 7 i (Schools) was issued by the DES as a supplement to the annual return of all pupils completed by head teachers. In Form 7 i 'immigrants were defined as:

1. Children born outside the British Isles who have come to this country with or to join parents whose country of origin was abroad.
2. Children born in the United Kingdom to parents whose country of origin was abroad and who came to the United Kingdom on or after 1st January 19   . (Ten years before the date of the collection of statistics.)

This definition, however, soon gave rise to a number of anomalies. The transition from 'immigrant' to 'non-immigrant' status for British born children was apparently to be determined by the parents' length of stay and unrelated to educational needs. Thus the reduction of children 'unable to follow a normal school curriculum with profit to themselves' from 25 to 16 per cent between 1967 and 1970 was likely to be a function, in part at least, of the smaller number of children classified as 'immigrant' at the later date. It soon became clear that it did not provide a means of measuring the needs of schools for language teaching, and the collection of statistics ceased in 1972. Margaret Thatcher's statement as Secretary of State for Education and Science in June 1973, that her department had 'made no use of them whatsoever except to publish them' appeared to confirm that no attempt had been made to draw upon or use the statistics to inform official policy.

Nevertheless the need for accurate statistical information remained urgent. The 1965 feasibility study of local authority policy and teaching practice in individual schools, undertaken for the Schools Council by June Derrick, was never published. However, Hawkes (1966) had attempted a survey of local and national policy based on local press, correspondence and personal contacts and, also in 1966, *Education* journal had undertaken a survey of local practices with the help of some 36 education officers in various part of the country. The climate of opinion created by these independent initiatives may well have been highly instrumental in the DES decision to fund a series of projects based at the National Foundation for Educational Research (NFER). The first survey resulted in the publication of *Immigrants in England: the LEA response* (Townsend, 1971) which concentrated on the administrative provisions of local education authorities to meet the needs of schools with immigrant pupils. This was followed by *Organisation in Multiracial Schools* (Townsend & Brittan, 1972) which dealt with the organisational measures in a sample of multiracial schools, and *Multiracial Education: need and innovation* (Townsend & Brittan, 1973) which was designed to investigate teachers' views on syllabuses, and the need to identify development and innovation in this aspect of education. The findings of these three surveys have had important implications for the formulation of language and other policies relating to the education of non-English speaking children.

Townsend & Brittan (1972), for instance, confirmed the special difficulties that had been created for both non-English speaking children and schools by the acute shortage of specialist teachers of English as a second language. The comment of one head teacher drew attention to the extremely unsatisfactory arrangements at which some schools arrived:

> There seems little doubt that many immigrant pupils are placed with less able pupils because of language difficulties. There is a danger that at this stage the progress of the immigrants will be unduly retarded because of the effects of pupil and teacher expectations on pupils' performance (Townsend & Brittan, op.cit.: 29)

The situation which the NFER reports outlined clearly pointed to the need for further and more accurate information than was currently available. Predictably, the decision in 1972 to cease the collection of educational statistics relating to children's ethnic origin caused considerable controversy for a number of years. It was felt that valuable opportunities were being lost both for informing government policy and for quantifying and locating particular needs (cf. Bullock, 1975: HMSO, 1977). A. Rampton (1981) recommended that from 1st September 1982 all schools should record the ethnic origin of a child's family on school entry and that the DES should reincorporate the collection of information on ethnic origin of pupils in its annual statistical exercise and introduce ethnic classification into its school leavers' survey.

In the meantime the most significant initiative in this area has been undertaken by the ILEA who decided in 1978 to provide a linguistic map of schools in their authority. Prior to the collection of statistics they had expressed anxiety that the volume of specialist teaching had been determined 'by overt demand rather than need, some of which may be latent' (ILEA, 1977: 10). The first census largely confirmed this suspicion, revealing that both the number and proportion of pupils not fully competent in English were found to vary considerably between divisions. The ILEA has also demonstrated the importance of updating information. Between 1978 and 1981, for instance, the number of Bengali speaking children in London increased by at least 50 per cent and Bengali overtook Greek as the language apart from English with most speakers. It has now been decided to institute a biennial language census to monitor the changing school population and its varying needs.

Second stage language teaching

Three surveys were published by the DES in the early 1970s. The first, *Potential and Progress in a Second Culture* (DES, 1971a) dealt with the attainment and assessment of intelligence in immigrant pupils. The second, *The Education of Immigrants: Education Survey 13* (1971b), was concerned with general policies and practices in the education of immigrant children and made it clear that the official views on dispersal had undergone some modification since the 1965 White Paper. The third, *The Continuing Needs of Immigrants* (1972) concentrated on the need for special help beyond the initial stage of English teaching and drew attention to the fact that only one LEA had consciously evolved a policy on the continuing linguistic needs of immigrants. Stress was laid on the importance of having 'much more positive thinking and constructive action in matters relating to the linguistic, intellectual and social needs of second phase immigrant pupils'.

The whole area of progression from initial to second stage language teaching was extremely problematic. For many years there was an absence of any objective way of assessing the level of proficiency after which schools could decide that no special arrangements were necessary. The first battery of tests of proficiency in English, for instance, were not available from the NFER until 1973. The most lucid exposition of this general area is contained in the chapter on 'Children from families of overseas origin' in the 1975 Bullock Report, *A Language for Life*. The expressed aim of initial language teaching which recurred in LEA policy statements at this time was to bring the child to a level at which 'he could profit from the normal school curriculum'. In practice, the time scale considered necessary to achieve this end varied between 12 and 18 months. There was a growing recognition, however, that such a short period was inadequate and that some form of continuing support for second stage learners was necessary:

> Although after a year he may seem able to follow the normal school curriculum, especially where oral work is concerned, the limitations to his English may be disguised; they become immediately apparent where he reads and writes. He reads slowly and often without a full understanding of vocabulary and syntax, let alone the nuances of expression. His writing betrays his lack of grasp of the subject and a very unsteady control of syntax and style... We regard it as a grave disservice to such children to deprive them of sustained language teaching after they have been learning English for only a comparatively short time. In our view they need far more intensive help with langue in English lessons. This should be the task of a specialist language teacher, whose aim should be to help them achieve fluency in all the language skills (Bullock, op.cit.: 290).

The ILEA has further recognized a third stage of language learning in which pupils show few signs of non-native use in spoken and written language, but none the less lack the full range of skills utilized by native speakers of the same age and ability. No survey has been undertaken to date of second or third stage provision. Its extent and kind is likely to vary considerably from one authority to another, and detailed policy statements would appear to be something of a rarity. It is difficult to estimate, therefore, the response to the Bullock Report's recommendation that language teachers in multiracial schools should be consultants and advisers across the curriculum rather than confined to a single room:

> As a matter of urgency teachers able to work in this way should be appointed extra to complement wherever secondary schools have on roll a significant number of children who are no longer classed as initial learners but need linguistic help (Bullock op.cit.: 291).

Recent developments and controversies in the teaching of English as a second language.

Several issues relating to the teaching of children for whom English is a second language have emerged as discussion points in recent years. One such issue concerns the role of teachers as language assessors, as is required, for instance, in the ILEA classification into second and third stage learners. This is a subject which has received very little attention in a British context. However, Shuy (1977), in a discussion of the American situation, makes a number of observations which may apply equally in the United Kingdom:

> In the US in the past we have relied on teacher assessments of the child's ability to speak English. Any analysis of such information, however, can demonstrate many errors... we can cite many examples such as that of the Mexican-American community in Lansing, Michigan, where the children are said to be fluent in English even though they are by far the lowest achievers in language related school subjects such as reading, spelling, writing and speech. The school's inability to assess children's language abilities is also evident from demographic analyses. In Fairfax County, Virginia, for example, 10% of the school population is Black, yet 90% of the children identified in that county as educably mentally retarded are Black. The San Francisco school records show practically no Chinese Americans as deaf while most of the educably mentally retarded are native Spanish speakers.

After reviewing a number of specific investigations, Shuy concludes:

> It is not easy to assess the language ability of a student and... accurate assessments of an individual's ability will best be made by a professional.

Shuy's comments should not have the effect of invalidating all teacher insights and observations on children's language. They do draw attention to the fact, however, that teachers *as a group* are sometimes linguistically naive and should not therefore be expected to give unguided assessments of children's language ability.

A second issue concerns 'second stage' English and the descriptions of 'deceptive fluency' which often accompany it. Various aspects of this discussion are widely accepted as fact, but have never been closely scrutinized. M. Rampton (1981), for instance, points to the notable absence of detailed descriptions of the language behaviour of bilingual children which would enable one to define linguistic criteria for such a condition, so that statements which refer to 'deceptive fluency' are necessarily impressionistic. He also suggests that any departures from the behaviour of native speakers might be attributed, in part at least, to the teaching strategies adopted with bilingual children. Because teachers are encouraged to converse with these children as observers rather than as participants, often concentrating more on the form of what they say than the content, they may not be experiencing the same range of language as indigenous pupils. Ironically, whereas teachers of English have been encouraged to adjust the language of the school in the direction of the pupil, teachers of English as a second language have tended to help the pupils with the linguistic demands of curriculum materials. A marked move from this position is to be observed in the work of writers like Wiles (1981) and Levine (1982) and projects such as BUF reported in Chapter Three. There is also an increasing number of practitioners who recognize the need to exploit the whole range of classroom interaction, and Chapters Six, Seven and Eight contain many examples of ways in which this can be achieved.

The final issue concerns the relationship between the specialist language teacher and the class teacher. Now that the majority of second language learners are British born the emphasis has inevitably moved from 'immigrant reception centres' withdrawing children for English teaching, to specialist staff working in conjunction with teachers in the normal school setting. There has been a growing understanding that the general classroom often provides a more meaningful context for learning English than a withdrawal group situation and that the skills needed to help children in their learning of English should be part of the professional competence of all teachers working in multilingual classrooms. Research evidence certainly provides some justification for this development. Fathman (1976), for instance, shows that those children who learn English exclusively or mainly in special withdrawal classes do not do as well as those who spend most of their time in ordinary classes.

This shift in emphasis often requires a reappraisal of classroom organization and teaching strategies for teachers who have received little or no training in working with second language learners, so that co-operation with specialist staff is both necessary and fruitful. The ILEA 'Second Language in the Primary School Project' (SLIPP) also recognizes the needs of classroom teachers in this area and has been developing materials which will allow them to support the learning of English through collaborative learning activities. Available at the time of writing are two video cassette programmes for teachers, from the ILEA 'Language in the Multiethnic Primary School' project, which focus on learning English as a second language. The first, 'Working Together in the Classroom', shows two boys collaborating on a maths task, a teacher working with a small group to interpret a chart they have made, and the children working independently. The second, 'Supporting understanding', shows children with little experience of English participating in science investigation and a maths activity. A teacher introduces and plays a game with a group of young children, and recordings show how individual children take a story as the starting point for a range of related activities. Other materials are currently in preparation.

Summary

The arrival in British schools throughout the 1960s and early 1970s of large numbers of children who spoke no English, posed serious philosophical, organizational and pedagogical problems for an education system which was unmistakably monolingual and monocultural. Central government offered little guidance and the autonomy of LEAs led to a vast array of responses which varied from total inertia ('They'll pick up English in the playground') to serious attempts to come to terms with a very difficult problem. For many years, however, there was little sharing of information or resources.

Because of progressively more restrictive immigration control there are now very few non-English speaking new arrivals in schools, though there are still many children who start nursery and reception classes speaking only the mother tongue. There has been a gradual recognition of the importance of collecting accurate information on the numbers and linguistic background of bilingual children and the precise nature of their language learning needs. There has also been a considerable change in attitudes towards bilingualism. Previously, bilingualism was felt to constitute an educational handicap and all efforts were directed at producing fluent English speakers using exclusively English medium methods. Such methods not only tended to produce an unnecessary emphasis on form over content, but overlooked positive benefits of using the children's mother tongues which will be explored in Chapter Three.

3 Bilingualism and the mother tongue issue

Throughout the 1960s and early 1970s English language teaching remained an unquestioned priority in the education of children for whom English was a second language. Since the late 1970s, however, considerable pressure has grown for the recognition and development of the first languages of the various ethnic minorities, and initiatives both inside and outside normal school hours have multiplied at an impressive rate. The debate which has grown up around what has come to be known as 'the Mother Tongue issue' deserves careful attention, not least because it challenges many assumptions very widely held in educational circles.

The community response

It has been estimated that approximately half of the ethnic minority children in our schools have a mother tongue other than English (Bullock, 1975). Yet we know very little of what precisely bilingualism entails for these children and their families. How important is it to linguistic minority communities to maintain their mother tongues? What steps do they take to ensure that the mother tongue is transmitted to their children? Is there evidence of language shift from one generation to the next? Do second and third generation children welcome efforts to preserve the mother tongue or do they resist them? Our knowledge of these areas tends to be sketchy, but some preliminary studies do give indications of likely answers to these questions.

First hand accounts from linguistic minority communities offer valuable insights into the different stages of awareness through which they have passed over a number of years. Hari Sewak, head teacher of a Punjabi Sunday school run by the Gudwara Singh Sabha in Slough, describes the feelings of the Asian communities thus:

> Asian parents are very anxious that Hindi, Urdu, Punjabi and Gujarati should be kept alive in their children. But in the early days they were busy with buying houses and had other such preoccupations on their minds. They were not articulate enough to ask for mother tongue teaching in the

school curriculum, and the communities were not yet well organised enough to arrange temple or mosque classes.... At the same time children were being strongly discouraged from using their mother tongues...in language units and in schools.... At first Asian parents did not object to these attitudes and approaches in schools, for they recognized that English is commercially more valuable in the country in which they have chosen to live. However, when children grew into their teens, and started to lose the common language of the home, parents became more anxious. They could not follow the English of their teenage sons and daughters, and there were many disputes.... Many parents began openly to demand action within their own communities. (Sewak, 1982)

Various small scale studies have been undertaken on attitudes towards language use among adults in linguistic minority communities (e.g. Bell, 1978; the Indian Welfare Association Wolverhampton survey reported in L. Mercer, 1981; Ghuman, 1980), but Wilding (1982) gives perhaps the fullest picture to date in her survey of families of Gujarati origin in Leicester. Parents in the sample were shown to be multilingual. All of them still speak their first language and most of them can read and write in it. There is a strong allegiance to the first language which is the main language used in the home and with the children and is also used extensively outside the home. A high proportion of the sample could speak and understand others in English and also read and write it. However, a quarter of the sample experienced communication difficulties outside the home, and there was a general recognition of the importance of English.

Nearly all of the respondents' children learnt an Asian language as their first language and most could still speak it. But whereas nearly all of the children could read and write English, very few were literate in the Asian language. Although few parents have actually sent their children to classes to learn their first language, the majority expressed a wish for them to attend such classes if facilities were available. The majority would also like their children to learn an Asian language at home and take a public examination. The Linguistic Minorities Project Adult Language Use Survey (see p.19) should neatly complement and expand the Leicester study. Considerably more ambitious than any previous study, it involved a team of 68 bilingual interviewers from seven different language groups interviewing a total of nearly 1,000 people. Results will be available in 1984.

Observations contained in the Wilding study concerning the parents' wish that children should be literate in the mother tongue can also be usefully supplemented by findings from the Rosen & Burgess (1980) survey. They found *prima facie* evidence of substantial numbers of children who had some facility in reading and writing a language other than English. This ability was, however, distributed differentially across the various linguistic minorities. Literacy was found to be high for speakers of Cantonese, Bengali, Arabic and Urdu, but relatively low for speakers of Gujarati, Punjabi and Hindi. They conclude:

> Education and other provision (the school and the local library, for example) needs to take some account of the degree to which literacy in the mother tongue is being maintained, not merely overall but in separate language communities. (p.74)

By far the most important index of community support for language maintenance, however, is the mushrooming of voluntary 'supplementary' schools teaching minority languages outside school hours. By the late 1960s and early 1970s the number of such schools had rapidly increased but still could not meet community demand (Saifullah Khan, 1976; 1980). The variation in these schools was considerable. Italian, Spanish and Portuguese embassies organized networks of classes centrally, while Gujarati, Chinese, Bengali and many other minority groups made uncoordinated locally-based provision. Some classes placed main or exclusive emphasis on religious teaching; others attached importance only to the maintenance of oral skills; still others aimed to make children literate in the mother tongue. Most mainstream school teachers and many LEAs knew very little about the extent and organization of this community provision and even today are not necessarily fully informed (cf. Tosi, 1979). By 1976 the demand for Mother Tongue Teaching (MTT) was so great and the voluntary classes were sufficiently well organized for the National Committee on Mother Tongue Teaching (NCMTT) to be formed as a channel through which information on the educational and cultural benefit of mother tongues other than English can be disseminated in Britain.

Attitudes of second and third generation settlers
Rather less information is available on the attitudes of second and third generation settlers to the mother tongue than on the feelings of their immigrant parents. It would seem, however, that a wide range of responses is to be found among this group of children and young people. Mercer, Mercer & Mears (1979), for instance, studied a group of 29 male and 9 female Gujaratis at a sixth form college and a college of further education in Leicester. The majority expressed an interest in supporting and maintaining Indian culture; most also considered Gujarati to be important in their social lives, particularly

in communication with monoglot elders. The group was very much divided, however, as regards the question of identity and attitudes towards the maintenance of Gujarati. Predictably, those who considered themselves as unambiguously Indian were very positively orientated towards the mother tongue while those who opted for a British identity tended to be relatively uninterested.

Another small scale study (Garton, 1980) also points to somewhat differing aspirations *vis-à-vis* the mother tongue. Garton administered a questionnaire on language usage and proficiency in English and Punjabi to some 44 Sikh children between the ages of 12 and 16 in Slough. Strong English language dominance emerged in both home and school domains. This was particularly marked in the case of boys aged between 14 and 16 who showed consistently low mean scores on measures of identification with Sikh culture and mother tongue. A highly significant correlation was in fact established between the degree of religious belief expressed and self-reports of language usage and proficiency, which would suggest that religion is a maintenance-prone domain for this sample. Garton suggests that, in terms of language maintenance, Punjabi is unlikely to survive as the mother tongue for the children of the respondents in this sample, except for limited use in religious contexts, and considers that greater efforts will be needed for Punjabi to survive.

The school response to Mother Tongue Teaching (MTT)

The suggestion that the mother tongues of ethnic minority children should be incorporated into the normal school curriculum was at first met with widespread incredulity in the teaching profession. This is not simply because of the central place occupied by English teaching, but also because of the tendency to undervalue bilingualism in children of South Asian origin. One head teacher consulted by Townsend (1971), for instance, commented:

> The Community Relations Officer thinks we should be teaching Gujarati but we couldn't start that caper. I've thought of starting French but we haven't enough space. (p.60)

A perceptible change of attitude towards minority languages on the part of the educational establishment, however, was to be observed in Bullock (1975):

> ... In a linguistically conscious nation in the modern world we should see (bilingualism) as an asset, as something to be nurtured, and one of the agencies which should nurture it is the school. Certainly the school should adopt a positive attitude to its pupils' bilingualism and wherever possible should help maintain and deepen their knowledge of their mother tongue. (p.293-4)

Unfortunately no indication was given in the Bullock report as to how, precisely, bilingualism should be promoted in the school.

Any discussion of the school response to bilingual pupils needs to take into consideration the organizational and political pressures produced by large scale migration which have been outlined in Chapter Two. It is also important to understand the controversy which has long surrounded bilingualism and the effect which this is likely to have had on the attitudes and practice of many teachers. The whole thrust of the educational establishment has been the teaching of English as a second language and underachievement has frequently been attributed to the child's inability to communicate on a par with the native English speakers. This interpretation, labelled by some writers (e.g. Ryan, 1976) as 'Blaming the Victim' can, however, be seen to be unduly narrow. Cummins (1981) neatly encapsulates the circular logic of this position in the table reproduced overleaf.

Bilingualism has long been regarded with some suspicion by educationalists. There has been a widespread feeling that the brain has only a finite capacity and bilingual children learn neither language as well as if they had restricted themselves to one language. Bilingualism is thus seen as something of an intellectual handicap. A large number of studies undertaken between 1920 and 1960 reported that bilingual children tended to perform more poorly in school than their monolingual peers, that they scored lower on the verbal parts of IQ tests and showed more emotional problems (see Darcy, 1953 and Peal & Lambert for overviews of these studies). However, there were often serious weaknesses in the design of this research. In some studies, working class bilingual children from under-resourced schools in poor areas were compared with middle class monolinguals. Other studies have taken no account of the fact that one language is usually dominant in bilingual speakers and have compared verbal scores on tests of children's weaker language with those of monolingual pupils.

Certainly there are some groups of bilingual children who do underperform in school. It is highly significant, however, that these children tend to belong to immigrant and minority language groups in the process of assimilation by a dominant majority group. Bilingualism in majority language groups, on the other hand, is considered to be an asset rather than a problem. In Canada, for instance, Anglophone children taking part in French 'immersion programs' who have been instructed mainly through the medium of French, suffer no adverse academic or cognitive consequences and catch up with English-medium control groups after English is

Table 2: Blaming the victim in minority language education

A. *Overt aim*	*Covert aim*	D. *Outcomes*	
Teach English to minority children in order to create a harmonious society with equal opportunity for all	Anglicize minority children because linguistic and cultural diversity are seen as a threat to social cohesion	—Even more intense efforts by the school to eradicate the deficiencies inherent in minority children	–The failure of these efforts only serves to reinforce the myth of minority group deficiencies
B. *Method*	*Justification*	C. *Results*	*'Scientific' explanation*
Prohibit use of L1 in schools and make children reject their own culture and language in order to identify with majority English group	1. L1 should be eradicated because it will interfere with the learning of English 2. Identification with L1 culture will reduce child's ability to identify with English-speaking culture	1. Shame in L1 language and culture 2. Replacement of L1 by L2 3. School failure among many children	1. Bilingualism causes confusion in thinking, emotional insecurity and school failure 2. Minority group children are 'culturally deprived' (almost by definition since they are not Anglos) 3. Some minority language groups are genetically inferior (common theory in the US in 1920s and 1930s)

L1=first language.
L2=second language.

Source: Cummins (1981) p.134

introduced at the ages of 8-9 (Genesee, 1979; Lambert & Tucker, 1972). Similarly, the general performance of children from English speaking homes who are taught increasingly through the medium of Welsh as they progress through the primary school, has been shown to compare very favourably with that of children in the exclusively English medium control schools (Evans, 1978).

The view that areas of ability are separate in each of a speaker's languages and that as each area develops less room is left for the other, is clearly inconsistent with the notable successes of French Canadian and Welsh bilingual education experiments, and alternative explanations must be sought. Cummins (1981), for instance, while recognizing that the surface forms of a bilingual's language are very different, proposes that there is a dimension of language usage, strongly related to literacy and other decontextualized verbal academic tasks, which he calls 'cognitive/academic language proficiency' or 'CALP'. He argues that there is considerable evidence from correlational studies that measures of CALP in both of a bilingual's languages are interdependent and must therefore be seen as manifestations of a common underlying proficiency.

Recognition that bilingualism does not necessarily constitute an educational disadvantage has thus been slow. It has certainly not been helped in Britain by a marked indifference to the learning of other languages and a sense of the importance of English as an international language. A hierarchy of preferences does, however, emerge in our attitudes towards other languages. The child who comes back from a lengthy stay in Europe speaking French or German or Spanish is considered to be very fortunate and is encouraged to make efforts to maintain fluency in that language. The bilingualism of the British born Asian child, in contrast, is either undervalued or ignored. L. Mercer (1981) reports that teachers have even been overheard admonishing children speaking Gujarati to each other at break time to 'stop jabbering'. She also points out that:

> For most British Asian children today home and school remain different language worlds and by the time they reach secondary school they may understandably have come to the conclusion that the language of their community is of no relevance to education... There can be little doubt that many Asian children are made to feel that their Indian language, the language of their ancestors, intimately tied up with traditional religion and custom, is second-rate, unworthy of educational attention. (p.152)

The considerable ambivalence among second and third generation members of linguistic minority communities reported above certainly lends support to this position.

The Council of the European Community's (EC) Directive on the Education of the Children of Migrant Workers

Strong pressure in relation to MTT has also resulted from the attention which has been paid in Europe since the mid-1970s to the linguistic education of migrants' children (Council of Europe, 1975a, b; European Communities Commission, 1976). This led to the circulation of the draft of the EC Directive to interested bodies in the United Kingdom in 1976. The response to proposals which had received little or no prior discussion in a British context was predictably hostile. Teacher organizations objected on the grounds that expansion in the area of MTT was unacceptable in the face of educational cutbacks and teacher unemployment. The Government objected on the grounds of cost, difficulty in providing teachers and inability of a decentralized education system to implement the Directive.

. When the EC Directive finally appeared in July 1977, important modifications had been made. Article 2, which referred to the need for member states to offer free tuition in the national language, and article 3 which referred to the teaching of the mother tongue and culture of migrants' children, had both been qualified with the words 'in accordance with their national circumstances and legal systems' (Council of Europe, 1977). Further, although it had originally been envisaged that the mother tongue and culture should form part of the curriculum for full time education with classes up to the normal standard for member states, the revised Directive simply called for member states to 'promote' MTT. The Directive thus does not confer any entitlement on individuals to tuition in school and stands in marked contrast to the North American Acts which instituted bilingual education.

There were also very real problems posed by the definition of 'migrant workers'. The strict interpretation of the Directive would in fact have constituted a violation of the Race Relations Act of 1976, since MTT would have been provided for children of workers from EEC member states but not for those from other linguistic minorities. However, a subsequent Council statement, public declarations from the Secretary of State for Education (cf. CRE, 1980) and the DES Circular 5/81 (July 31st, 1981) have all made it clear that the Directive will be applied to member state nationals and British ethnic minorities alike. It is unfortunate that the term 'migrant worker' has been retained, since a primary motive of the Directive in the European continental context is to facilitate children's 'possible reintegration into the Member State of origin' (Council of Europe, 1977). There have been calls for the retitling of the Directive and for the DES to state clearly and publicly that the reintegration of minority groups is not one of the aims of MTT.

While the EC Directive is legally binding on member states, considerable scepticism has been expressed about government willingness or ability to achieve even the modest aims set out in the revised version. As Bellin (1980) points out:

There are so many ways in which a member state government can be let off the hook. It is possible to plead difficulties with national circumstances, problems with conforming to the legal system, and there is always the excuse that, however little is being done, almost anything can count as 'promoting mother tongue teaching'.

MTT projects and materials

The extent of the DES commitment to date has been limited to the funding of three projects related directly or indirectly to MTT. The first was a study of linguistic diversity in a sample of London secondary schools (Rosen & Burgess, 1980). The second concerned Punjabi children entering two schools in Bradford in the term before their fifth birthday with little or no English; one group was taught equally in both English and Punjabi, the other almost exclusively in English. Children's progress and school and community attitudes were monitored. Results to date indicate that children taught through both Punjabi and English performed on a par with the control group in English tasks and at a superior level in Punjabi (Rees et al., 1981). Thirdly, the Linguistic Minorities Project (1978-82) aimed to establish the range of linguistic diversity in all schools in a small number of LEAs, to collect information on all forms of mother tongue provision in a few areas and to undertake more limited studies of language use by adults.

Two projects sponsored by the European Community can also be conveniently mentioned at this point. The Bedford Mother Tongue Project took place in Bedford in 1976-80 and was designed to investigate the educational implications of teaching children of Italian and Punjabi background the language, history, geography, music, games and social studies of their families' country of origin. There is also the Schools Council Mother Tongue Project which aims to develop materials for bilingual teachers of Greek and Bengali speaking pupils in the 7-11 age range, to develop a strategy for producing materials which may be applicable to other languages, and to produce guidelines for monolingual teachers working in linguistically diverse classrooms across the whole primary age range.

Finally, ILEA initiatives in the area of mother tongue teaching should be considered. In addition to funding ten schemes teaching mother tongue languages outside school hours, ILEA has been responsible for the development of two sets of bilingual materials for normal classroom use. The first, *The World in a City*, is a pack of 40 cards available in eight different language combinations with English, and aimed at students already literate in their first language who are in the process of learning English as a second or third language. The second, *Face Play*, inset puzzles, has been produced by Bilinguals Under Five (BUF), a project set up to consider ways of supporting young children learning English as a second language within the normal pre-school framework. The puzzles aim to provide material for small groups of children working together, encouraging them to explore the similarities and differences of faces in a sensitive and positive way. The BUF project has also produced a series of four 30 minute video programmes called *Working with Young Bilingual Children*, which explore ways in which the nursery environment can build on the linguistic and cultural resources of children in the wider community to support their linguistic and cognitive development.

Approaches and controversies in MTT

Whatever the weaknesses of the EC Directive it has achieved the effect of stimulating considerable debate. It is interesting to note, however, that MTT can be supported from a number of quite different and sometimes conflicting perspectives and there is growing awareness of the importance of making explicit one's starting point in commending it. Participants at the September 1981 DES conference at Bedford College of Higher Education isolated six main ideologies for the teaching of the mother tongue:

1. *Child-centredness*
   The argument for MTT from this perspective is that it promotes self-esteem in the individual pupil; facilitates the expression of feeling and promotes emotional growth; diminishes the gap between the culture of the home and the culture of the school; and promotes the well-being of the individual child within his or her own family and community. (For example, on this latter point, MTT helps the child to maintain contact with parents and grandparents, and access to religious writings and worship.) Feeling both more secure and more highly motivated, the child makes better academic progress at school.

2. *Integration*
   The argument for MTT is that it facilitates the learning of, and switch to, English and assimilation into British society. With regard to the 15-18 age group a further integrationist argument – that is, an argument relating to the wish to integrate minority groups fully into mainstream society – is that MTT can add to a pupil's GCE qualifications, and help him or her to get a better, more influential job. Further, MTT may contribute to mainstream society's export drive, and to the operations of extractive industries in certain other countries.

3. *Liberalism*
   The argument for MTT is that the person who knows two or more languages has greater insight into reality and into his or her own self,

and greater access to the wisdom and insight of other human beings, than the monolingual person. The greater a person's understanding of self and environment, the more he or she is able to exercise personal choice; to mould the environment to his or her own values, interests and desires; and to respect the rights of others similarly to exercise personal choice. MTT contributes, in short, to the promotion and maintenance of democracy.

4. *Radicalism*
   The argument for MTT is that it promotes cohesion and solidarity within minority communities. Therefore it enables them to defend themselves better against groupings and tendencies in mainstream society which threaten them, and enables them to organize themselves more effectively to press and work for greater equality and justice.

5. *Maintaining traditional relationships*
   The argument for MTT is that it helps to maintain (through the pedagogy which is adopted as well as through the content) traditional relationships and attitudes between the generations, and between the sexes; it maintains the authority and influence of the older generation in relation to the younger, and of male in relation to female. MTT may also be linked to conservative or traditional political groupings in the country of origin of minority communities.

6. *Racism*
   The argument for MTT is that it facilitates eventual repatriation – both in the sense that minority groups can be expected to settle more readily in another country if they have learnt that country's language, and also, perhaps much more importantly, because MTT can demonstrate to mainstream public opinion that minority groups do not 'belong'. MTT also has the advantage, from a racist perspective, of distracting minority groups from pressing for more fundamental changes in society and in education; and in classes and schools run by minority groups themselves, MTT conveniently contributes to social control of teenagers and young people (Halliday, 1981: 1-2).

Given the highly conflicting nature of some of these positions it is perhaps not surprising that considerable controversy has grown up around the subject of MTT. Some observers, e.g. Brook (1980) argue that MTT may operate more effectively as a means of controlling ethnic minority populations than promoting cultural diversity. It has also been argued that if separate arrangements are made for MTT within a school this may have the effect of creating an apartheid-like situation which may ultimately have an adverse effect on minority pupils' achievement. However, supporters of MTT of non-racist and non-assimilationist persuasions (see, for example, *Issues in Race and Education*, No. 35), argue that, providing schools and teachers are aware of the potential dangers, it is possible to take measures to avoid them. It is important, for instance, to ensure that parent's first languages are not used simply as one-way instruments of social control which allow the school to communicate its wishes to parents without taking note of parents' feelings and aspirations. Similarly, it is vital that mother tongue classes should not be timetabled to clash in any way with important subject options.

Whose responsibility?

It is by no means clear as to the extent of responsibility which should be taken by the state for teaching the mother tongues of linguistic minorities. A survey undertaken by the Indian Welfare Association in 1979 in Wolverhampton (reported in L. Mercer, 1981), for instance, showed that some 81 per cent of the 1,000 parents interviewed wanted their children to learn their mother tongue as part of their normal school curriculum. Only 45 per cent of the Punjabi families in Cardiff interviewed by Ghuman (1980), however, supported this position; the others considered that MTT should be undertaken by the community and, in particular, by the Gudwara.

Nor is it simply a question of a dichotomy between school and community. If teaching takes place in school, should it be inside or outside the timetable, and optional or compulsory? If it takes place in the minority communities, should it be with or without the financial and moral support of local education authorities, and with or without formal liaison with mainstream schools (cf. Halliday, 1981)? These possibilities are not, of course, mutually exclusive, and there is room for considerable variation in provision depending on the needs and wishes of the minority communities involved. It would seem, however, that some kind of LEA support is essential. L. Mercer (op.cit.) reports that only 11 per cent of ethnic minority children in Leicester attend supplementary schools, although the vast majority of parents expressed a wish to send their children to such schools if places were available. For this reason alone, Mercer argues:

> State schools cannot justifiably leave the educational treatment of an important area of their pupils' experience to voluntary institutions. (p.156)

The importance of consultation with minority communities cannot, however, be overemphasized. It is essential to recognize, for instance, that MTT does not always apply to the first language acquired by minority children. Many Italian parents in Britain do not consider themselves as permanent residents and would be likely to show a strong preference for their children to be taught standard Italian, a variety very different from the Southern dialect which most of them speak, so as to equip them for reintegration into schools at home. By the same token, Punjabi speaking Pakistani parents prefer their children to learn Urdu, the language of religion and 'high culture'. As Tosi (1979) points out:

> Involving minority groups in policy decisions is not only due recognition of their 'adulthood' but also a guarantee of correctly interpreting the social and linguistic orientation of their neighbourhood. (p.276)

Various pressure groups are actively campaigning for the provision of MTT within the state educational system and detailed policy statements have been prepared by the National Committee for Mother Tongue Teaching (NCMTT), the National Association for Multiracial Education (NAME) and the Commission for Racial Equality (CRE). Local authorities, too, are beginning to look closely at the MTT requirements of ethnic minority children within their schools and many have prepared their own policy statements (cf. Tsow, forthcoming).

The importance of the formulation of coherent language policies is underlined by the Welsh experience, where the rapid decline in the proportion of Welsh speakers has effectively been halted in the last decade (Bellin, 1983). This has been achieved by replacing ill-defined concern with careful clarification of aims, and a commitment to the aims at government, local authority and school levels (V. Edwards, 1984). It has also involved the development of methodologies and resources, and a sharing of knowledge and experience. In a wider British context, Rosen & Burgess (1980: 109) suggest a number of practical steps which could be taken without placing serious strains on existing resources and organization:

1. Local authorities should know which of their schools contain minorities in sufficient numbers to justify the consideration of mother tongue classes within the curriculum.

2. Local authorities should also compile a list of teachers who could teach minority languages or be trained to do so.

3. Schools should take the initiative in starting classes and ask for the financial and other resources to sustain them.

4. At all levels there is need to pool resources. There are too many lonely improvisers. The experience of other countries should be made available to teachers.

Bilingual education
Any discussion of MTT in a British context would be incomplete without reference to the wider international debate on bilingual

education. The precise form which bilingual education takes varies considerably both from country to country and within countries, but Fishman (1976) distinguishes four main approaches. The first - transitional bilingualism - makes use of both the mother tongue and the main language in the early years of school, but as soon as children are proficient in the main language the mother tongue is dropped. The next approach - monoliterate bilingualism - encourages the development of oral/aural skills in both languages, but promotes literacy in the main language of instruction and not in the mother tongue. Biliterate bilingualism, on the other hand, encourages literacy in both languages, though it is possible to make a distinction between partial biliterate programmes, in which literacy skills in the mother tongue are usually restricted to the study of the literature, history and culture of that language, and full biliterate programmes in which both languages are used equally as the medium of instruction.

In a British context, the Bradford Mother Tongue and English Teaching Project was a clear example of transitional bilingualism as, too, are the ILEA 'World in a City' and 'BUF' materials. Most bilingual projects in Wales and Scotland, in contrast, can be classified as partial biliterate programmes. Transitional bilingual projects have in fact been the object of a great deal of concern in some countries, particularly in America, where a number of observers (e.g. Fishman, 1976) consider they are merely subtle instruments of social control and are indicative of a compensatory approach to education (cf. 'Blaming the Victim', p.36). Indeed, bilingual education as a whole proved to be a very important political issue in the USA, where it has received considerably more financial and legislative backing than in Britain. Many extravagant claims were made for bilingual education (cf. Fishman, op.cit., MacNamara, 1974; J. Edwards, 1981b) but it has rapidly become clear that such programmes cannot in themselves compensate for the social and economic disadvantage which is frequently experienced by members of linguistic minorities. Proponents of bilingual education must therefore make it quite clear that its advantages lie in its potential for the promotion of mutual understanding and respect, rather than as a panacea for educational disadvantage.

Wright (1978) attempts to answer the question 'What should we do in Britain?' in terms of a bilingual education programme within the mainstream school, which is based on choices. Minority language/ culture groups should have the choice of maintaining their languages and cultural traditions as well as becoming fluent in the language and culture of the majority group. Only the pupils themselves can decide on the appropriate balance between languages and cultures. This should not, however, be a one-sided process and majority group children, too, should be offered the chance of learning something of the language and background of the minority groups in the school and neighbourhood. Wright proposes six criteria which can be used in a learning situation to evaluate the extent to which a particular activity will benefit minority group students and help rather than hinder the growth of mutual understanding and respect:

1. The motive for introducing minority languages into the learning situation must be utilitarian, not tokenist.

2. Integrate the work stimulated by minority language books/tapes/work cards etc. with the mainstream of class activity.

3. Provide within the classroom the opportunity of developing and refining the skills of bilingualism - translation and interpretation - not only of language but of cultural experience.

4. Provide language learning opportunities, and the opportunity of becoming bilingual, to all students - even though a very small minority of English speaking students would take up the option.

5. Never segregate the minority group for mother tongue learning... without explicitly inviting all pupils/students to join the group.

6. Preserve and defend the minority group student's right to choose for her/himself the balance of minority and majority group language and culture which best meets the desired identity of the individual.

Summary

It is obviously a matter of urgency that children entering school with little or no English should achieve fluency in English as rapidly as possible. In the early years of immigration it was felt that this could be achieved most efficiently by using the 'direct method' in which children's mother tongues played no part. More recently, however, the role of the mother tongue in children's linguistic and cognitive development has been recognized. There has also been a growing understanding of the importance of family relations and of the development of a strong sense of cultural identity. None the less, MTT remains a controversial issue: it can be commended from a number of perspectives, some of which are conflicting; and it is not always clear whether responsibility for classes should fall on school, community or both. MTT is thus an area which needs careful thought and organization, and the formulation of detailed policy statements by national bodies and local authorities is an encouraging development. Finally, the more specialized interests of MTT should not detract from the wider issue of bilingualism and the part which minority languages and cultures can play in the education of all children.

4 Language in the British Black community

Language in a Caribbean context

The mid 1960s saw the influx of large numbers of Caribbean settlers into the United Kingdom. They spoke a variety of English, completely unfamiliar to the majority of indigenous British people, which is known as 'Creole' by linguists but generally called 'patois' by West Indians themselves. When people from many parts of West Africa, speaking a wide range of different languages, were transported as slaves to the Caribbean, there was an urgent need to develop some common mode of communication. The simple pidgin evolved in the early years of slavery was developed into a full-blown language - or creole - by subsequent generations, and whereas the pidgin had served only rudimentary communication needs, the creole was expanded into a full and very adequate linguistic system. There are various differences from one West Indian territory to another, particularly in some aspects of vocabulary and intonation. There remains, however, a core of common grammatical features found in the speech of all or most of the islands (cf. V. Edwards, 1979; Sutcliffe, 1982). French creoles, spoken by Saint Lucian and Dominican settlers in Britain, bear the same relationship to French as English creoles do to English and, although the vocabulary base is different, they have much in common with the Caribbean English creoles.

A recurring question in discussions of West Indian language is whether Caribbean varieties should be classed as dialects of English or as a separate language. They are arguably further removed from standard English than any British dialect and writers like Sutcliffe (op.cit.) make a strong case for treating them separately. The distinction between 'language' and 'dialect' is, however, extremely hazy. The linguistic situation in Scandinavia, for instance, can most usefully be described as a continuum of dialects from Norway in the north to Denmark in the south. Yet Danes, Swedes and Norwegians form three distinct political units and are adamant that they speak three distinct languages. Relatively small linguistic differences assume considerable importance and help to define three separate national identities. The various dialects of the Arab world, on the other hand, are characterized by differences far greater than those held to delimit separate languages in Scandinavia. Strong ideals of religious and cultural unity, however, lead Arabs to minimize these differences. There are thus no clear or well-defined criteria for establishing whether we are dealing with a language or a dialect and ultimately the politician is in a better position to make such a decision than the linguist. Those wishing to promote a separate Jamaican identity, for example, might find it helpful to treat Jamaican Creole as a language quite distinct from the English associated with a colonial past.

Structure of West Indian Creoles

West Indian Creoles are perfectly regular, rule-governed linguistic systems which should properly be described in their own terms rather than by comparison with other systems such as standard English. Examples of such descriptions can be found in works like Bailey's (1966) *Jamaican Creole Syntax* and Sutcliffe's (1982) *British Black English*. For present purposes, however, I have chosen to outline the main contrasts between West Indian Creoles and English, emphasizing throughout that we are dealing with grammatical differences rather than deficiencies. This is not because I wish to fit West Indian language into an English mould, or to minimize the ways in which it functions quite autonomously, but simply because I recognize that English speakers will inevitably make comparisons between the two systems. There is a tendency to label any departures from the standard as 'inadequate' or 'incorrect' and so I feel that it is important to squarely challenge such assumptions.

Features of West Indian Creoles

1. Creole does not usually mark plural nouns as English does:
   > Me have three brother and two sister

   Here the number makes it obvious that we are dealing with plural nouns. But when Creole needs to show that it is referring to more than one person or thing and there are no plural words in the sentence, it uses 'de...-dem':
   > De girl-dem come here all the time

2. There is often no agreement between subject and verb:
   > The boy come in the morning
   > My brother go to work

   The English 's' for the third person singular is, in fact, a relic of an older system (e.g. thou givest) and is largely redundant.

3. The Creole verb does not inflect for tense:
    My mother come here yesterday
    I see John last week
Creole does, however, have another way of showing time relations.
    In Jamaican Creole we find:
    Mary a go home = Mary is going home
    ('a' shows that an action is in progress)
    John en go home = John went home
    ('en' shows that an action took place in the past)

4. Creole shows possession not with the genitive marker, 's' of British English, but by the relative positions of possessor and possessed:

British English	Creole
John's hat	John hat
The teacher's book	The teacher book

5. Pronouns only show person and number. They don't usually show case or gender. In Broad Jamaican Creole you find:

a. me	we
b. you	unu
c. him, it	dem

    Thus, you might have:
    me see him brother yesterday = I saw his/her brother yesterday
    unu make we go back = you let us go back

6. The verb 'to be' in Creole is largely redundant (compare also Russian). Both adjectives and verbs and, in some situations, nouns and locatives can follow the subject:
    Winston coming
    Winston good
    Winston the father

7. There is no separate passive form in Creole:
    The food eat quick = the food was eaten quickly
    The property sell = the property was sold

8. Some words and constructions common to Creole and British English have different meanings:
    Anne is easy to annoy = Anne annoys people easily
    Mind you don't go home = Be sure you go home

9. Some words and constructions are completely different:
    A walk me walk make me come so late = It's because I walked that I'm so late
    Me nyam all the food = I ate all the food

British Black Language

'West Indian' is a misleading and inaccurate label for the British born children and grandchildren of the original settlers in this country, many of whom have never set foot in the Caribbean. A distinctive British Black community is emerging which has retained many elements of West Indian language and culture, but which is also showing a high degree of innovation and adaptation.

Who speaks Creole?

Many teachers and other observers feel that most British Black children conform to local linguistic norms and sound like their white peers. Rosen & Burgess, for instance, included questions in their survey of the *Languages and Dialects of London School Children* which assessed the strength of dialect features in children's speech, and concluded on the basis of teacher estimates that between 80 and 90 per cent of children of West Indian origin are 'basically London (or standard) speakers who occasionally deepen overseas dialectal features'. As few as 10 to 20 per cent of these children regularly used Creole in certain contexts and less than 4 per cent used a 'full Caribbean creole'.

There is, however, a certain subjectivity in estimates of this kind which is highlighted by the very different results achieved by other researchers. Sutcliffe (1978), for instance, in a study of the language attitudes and use of some 47 first and second generation West Indians in Bedfordshire found that almost 95 per cent of subjects admitted using some Creole, and 78 per cent thought that they at least occasionally used Creole of a broadness equivalent to, *'mi aks di man fi put im money iina mi pockit'*. Hadi (1976) replicated this experiment in a West Midlands secondary school and found that over 70 per cent of her sample of 22 West Indian pupils admitted to using sentences like 'mi aks di man...'. In both cases, these researchers drew on children's own self-estimates in structured group interviews, having established their own positive attitudes towards Creole before beginning the interview by, for example, playing and discussing tapes of West Indian and other speech.

Palmer (1981) approached this question in two quite different ways. First she gave a well-motivated class teacher copies of the Rosen & Burgess questionnaire and discussed with him how it should be completed. When the questionnaires were returned, she visited the class herself and, after playing and discussing tapes of various languages and dialects, she withdrew small groups and administered the Sutcliffe questionnaire. She found that children's self-estimates of Creole usage were consistently higher than those of the teacher, although she had consulted the children before completing the questionnaire. Tomlin's (1981) study of a random sample of West Indian subjects in Dudley might also be mentioned at this point. 100 per cent of the people who took part in street interviews admitted to Tomlin, a black student teacher, that they regularly used Creole in some situations.

The discrepancy between the findings of Rosen & Burgess and the other researchers can undoubtedly be attributed to different methodologies. The low status of Creole is such that a certain degree of under-reporting is inevitable and it is interesting that a higher proportion of children admitted using Creole to researchers who presented themselves as friendly and interested adults than to teachers. This is not to suggest, of course, that teachers are either unfriendly or uninterested. However, their role as authority figures may well have affected children's responses. The actual questions which were asked may also go some way to explaining observed differences. The fact, for instance, that children were offered a specific example ('mi aks di man...') against which they could measure their own usage may well have given them more confidence to reply positively.

It is ironical that the use of teachers as researchers simultaneously represents the greatest strength and the greatest weakness of the Rosen & Burgess survey. They formed a tremendous pool of on-the-spot, interested and well-motivated researchers; their participation in the survey stimulated discussion and led ultimately to a realization of the exciting potential of linguistic diversity as a classroom resource. The use of teacher researchers, however, also led to what Rosen & Burgress (1980; 2-3) describe as 'a compromise between the delicacy of information we would have liked to obtain and what it would be reasonable to expect to collect with the assistance of teachers who made no special claim to expert knowledge'.

The Rosen & Burgess survey was made under difficult circumstances with limited funding and, without the use of teacher researchers, would have been a totally impractical exercise. A number of important questions, however, are raised by both results and methodology – how legitimate is it, for instance, to make use of labels as imprecise as 'occasionally deepens dialect features' or 'basically a London speaker'? None the less, the study is an important one in that it has started to document the nature and extent of diversity. Rosen & Burgess openly acknowledge its weaknesses and make no extravagant claims for its findings. Most important, they show something of the complexity of diversity and its centrality for education.

When is Creole used?

An adequate description of British Black language use requires more precision than the rather vague observation that most Black Britons can approximate to both the local white norm and more 'focused' Creole speech. Some investigation has been done on this subject but it relies heavily on either researcher speculation or British Black subjective judgements. It does appear, however, that British Black children are particularly sensitive to situation. Hadi (1976) asked first year children in a Walsall secondary school if they would change from the way they spoke to their friends when speaking to certain adults. The results show some very interesting tendencies:

Table 3: Self-estimates of language use in English and British Black Children

		British Black %	English %
Head teacher	No change	6	25
	Change	94	75
Doctor	No change	12	31
	Change	88	69
Milkman	No change	17	77
	Change	83	23
School dinner lady	No change	13	55
	Change	87	45

Source: extrapolated from Hadi (1976)

In all four cases a higher proportion of British Black than English children say they would change their speech. And, whereas the English children tend to discriminate between low and high status adults, the proportion of Black children who say they would change the way they speak remains uniformly high across all four groups. Hadi speculates as to whether this sensitivity to situation is an indication of insecurity on the part of Black children. It seems more probable, however, that since the British Black community has a wider range of language at its disposal, Black children are able to make an additional distinction which is not available to their English peers.

Hadi (op.cit) and Sutcliffe (1978, 1982) also challenge the long held assumptions about the simple split in West Indian language use whereby 'Creole' is spoken at home and 'English' at school. It emerged in the Sutcliffe study that subjects' own rate of use was highest in the peer group situation when talking to Black friends in the playground. Parents' use of Creole to children, however, is correspondingly high, though subjects' own use to parents is low. Scores for use to brothers and sisters tended to be intermediate to low. Hadi's findings were not as conclusive as those of Sutcliffe, but there was certainly general agreement that Creole was used widely to their friends at school and was often triggered by stress - anger, excitement, joy, playing cards, 'when there is a fight' or 'someone shout at me'.

The asymmetrical use of Creole reported in Sutcliffe (1978, 1982) is something which has not previously attracted comment in a British setting. Sutcliffe (1982), however, draws parallels with research on this phenomenon in both Black American and Caribbean communities. He suggests that the use of Creole is akin to the *tu* form in French, whereas more English usage is associated with the *vous* form. He points to a pattern in which younger people are expected to use 'English' to their parents and even older brothers and sisters, but parents and elders are allowed to use Creole to their juniors. A very similar situation prevailed with the use of *tu* and *vous* in France a generation or so ago. Interestingly, drama and literature emerging from the British Black community-in particular, *Jennifer and Brixton Blues* (Richmond, 1978) and *Ballad for You* (Johnson, 1978) - contain family dialogues which confirm Sutcliffe's observations.

Valuable information on the use of Creole outside the family is contained in Crump's (1979) study of the language of Black children in a Haringey mixed comprehensive school. She considers the importance of language as an integral part of a person's identity and relates the language varieties of Black adolescents to their involvement in particular youth cultures. Children's comments, together with observations of the classroom and the playground, suggest that it is only when pupils develop an orientation towards one or another of the major youth cultural groupings that differences in language become apparent. Those pupils who by the third and fourth years use patois and take pride in 'talking Black' are those who turn to the all Black world of reggae and sound systems. The strength of Crump's study lies in its sensitive and sympathetic handling of the situation of Black children in Britain. She does not, however, undertake any kind of linguistic analysis and children's speech appears only in quotations which illustrate the various points she makes in her sociological analysis.

Crump's observations are confirmed by various writers concerned with the sociological phenomenon presented by Black people in Britain rather than more directly linguistic considerations. Hebdige (1976), for instance, comments on the ways in which West Indian youths have developed Creole as a symbol of group identity:

> Language is used [by members of certain West Indian sub-cultures] as a particularly effective way of resisting assimilation and preventing infiltration by members of the dominant groups. As a screening device it has proved to be invaluable, and the 'Bongo talk' and patois of the Rude Boy deliberately emphasize its subversive rhythms so that it becomes an aggressive assertion of racial and class identities. As a living index of the extent of the Black's alienation from the cultural norms and goals of those who occupy high positions in the social structure the Creole language is unique.

Leitch (1979), from her position as an insider in the British Black community, argues that the language used by children of Caribbean origin in Britain varies very considerably depending on where in the Caribbean their family comes from; the social background of the family, how long they or their family have lived here, and, most important, the proportion of the people they associate with who are of Caribbean origin and speak a Creole, and the extent to which they identify with Caribbean or British culture. She suggests that the language of many of these children is influenced by the Creole or other language of the parents; peer group language; language of the school and media which may be the standard; London Jamaican; and Rastafarian terminology and structure.

Thomas (1979), like Leitch and Crump, does not undertake a linguistic analysis of children's speech, but offers nonetheless some interesting insights in an ethnographic report based on participant observational study in a multi-ethnic primary school. She develops the metaphorical construct of 'personal space' which she conceives in terms of 'territory' that can be infringed or vindicated by the interactional processes to which we are exposed. Thomas reports a wide range of Creole usage in the children in her school, from a few stock phrases copied from their mothers' rebukes or from pop songs to the ability to hold long conversations in patois. She examines the social significance of this Creole usage in the classroom, suggesting that Black pupils use Creole to reinforce group communication, to threaten an outsider to the group who violates their personal space, or to signify inclusion if they wish to vindicate an outsider.

Code switching

The linguistic situation of the British Black community would appear to differ from that of West Indians in the Caribbean in two main respects. First, it is frequently claimed that the vast majority of West Indians both understand and use Creole, whereas in Britain it is confined to a very small segment of the population. Second, most members of the British Black community are capable of producing a variety of English close to the local British norm and, in some cases, indistinguishable from it, whereas very few West Indians have a good command of the local standard English. The polar varieties which can be achieved by many Black Britons are thus, not surprisingly, much further apart than those of most West Indians in the Caribbean. The range of linguistic variation in the West Indies is usually described in terms of a dialect continuum (cf. V. Edwards, 1979), but it seems possible that the British Black situation can be better described in terms of a bilingual continuum.

One of the characteristics of British Black language use which is consistent with the notion that we are dealing with a bilingual community is the high degree of code-switching between Creole and English. This can take place from sentence to sentence:

I hate coffee. *mi laik tii.*

The duppy came and saw Brother Brown. *An di dopi snach di kaan.*

Yu gat rak stik iina yu hiez. You've got rocks sticking in your ears.

from clause to clause:

When me sister loses her temper *mi gaan so.*

and even from phrase to phrase:

and he did see... he did see the um... *di dopi*

and so the donkey *lif op* his leg

Why don't you come with me to the... *tu di griev*

Code switching of this kind is an extremely widespread phenomenon which has been documented for bilingual communities as far apart as Ghana (Ure, 1974), India (Kachru, 1978) and America (Hernandez-Chavez et al., 1975). It has been demonstrated that this switching is not random but subject to grammatical constraints and is triggered by a range of psychological variables, such as hesitation, and sociological variables, such as topic and audience. The discovery of such constraints is of considerable importance because it indicates that switching is not simply an inability to keep two languages apart but an extremely complex ability found in some bilinguals.

The recognition of this code-switching behaviour in the British Black community is extremely recent (cf. V. Edwards, 1982) and a great deal of work remains to be done before we can say with any degree of confidence what precisely is taking place. It would seem to indicate, however, that we have greatly underestimated the complexity of the linguistic situation of Black people in Britain. Educators have tended to view Black pupils either as linguistically assimilated or as linguistically lacking, in the case of those who continue to show Creole influence in their speech. It is very important, therefore, that we should understand the rule-governed nature of language behaviour and the symbolic role which Creole continues to play in the lives of many Black Britons, as well as the social mechanisms underlying the long-term survival of Creole.

The school response to the language of Black children

West Indian Creole speaking children arriving from the Caribbean posed a number of important questions which schools identified only slowly and on which central government provided little or no guidance for a disturbing period of time. Ignorance about the rule-governed nature of West Indian speech was widespread. A report by the National Association of Schoolmasters (NAS, 1969), for instance, considered that:

> The West Indian child usually arrives speaking a kind of 'plantation English' which is socially unacceptable and inadequate for communication. (p.5)

An ATEPO (1970) report describes West Indian language as 'babyish', 'careless and slovenly' and 'very relaxed like the way they walk'. Even Townsend (1971), who acknowledges the validity of West Indian children's language, talks of their 'abbreviated sentence structure, different pronoun values and restricted vocabulary'.

West Indians, for their part, had grown up in a society where the institutions, including education, were closely modelled on the British system. They had been indoctrinated into believing that West Indian Creoles were 'bad talk' and 'broken'. When they came to what many people regarded as 'the mother country', it was therefore understandable that they should insist that they spoke English, since to have admitted otherwise would have been tantamount to an acceptance of the low status attached to Creole speech. Problems concerning mutual intelligibility between West Indian parents and children on the one side and teachers on the other were common throughout the early years of settlement (cf. Rose et al., 1969; V. Edwards, 1979).

Any official recognition of the language needs of West Indian children was extremely slow, and DES statistics served to conceal rather than to draw attention to the true situation. Section Two of

Form 7i, a supplement to the annual statistical return made by schools which was introduced in 1966, required teachers to classify 'immigrant' children according to their knowledge of English as follows:

(i) No problem
(ii) Reasonably good spoken English but weak in written English
(iii) Some English, but needing further intensive teaching
(iv) No English

It seems reasonable to assume that if teachers were required to choose between either group (ii) or group (iii) when classifying West Indian children, they would come out in favour of group (ii) (cf. Power, 1967). Yet the following year the DES amalgamated groups (i) and (ii) and groups (iii) and (iv) on the assumption that only those children in groups (iii) and (iv) would require specialized language teaching. Such a move effectively excluded the possibility that West Indian children might need specialist help, albeit of a different nature from second language learners.

The actual arrangements for teaching West Indians reflect the unfortunate consequences of a lack of policy on either a national or a local level. Comments reported by Townsend & Brittan (1972), for instance, reveal the bewilderment and confusion which must have been experienced by teachers and pupils alike:

> We once arranged special coaching for West Indians whose English was very poor, but they tended to resent this, not accepting that there was anything wrong with their English, so little progress was made and the project abandoned. (p.26)

All too often the solution adopted with West Indian pupils (as with non-English speaking children) was to place them in classes with remedial indigenous children:

> Boys of West Indian origin: in each year we have a class for retarded pupils. Although not designed as such, all of these classes have about 90 per cent West Indians or pupils of West Indian origin. (p.26)

Only in a very few cases did schools or LEAs make any serious attempt to meet the language teaching needs of West Indian pupils (cf. Rose et al., 1969:281).

Large scale West Indian immigration predated migration from South Asia by several years. Yet it was not until 1967 that the Schools Council commissioned a project with aims similar to the Leeds project (see Chapter Two) but whose brief was to develop teaching materials specifically for West Indian pupils. Although the number of children who might benefit from such materials was probably no smaller than the number of non-English speaking children, the budget for this project was less than a third of that made available to the Leeds team. The *Concept 7-9* materials produced by the 'Teaching English to children of West Indian origin' research team (cf. Wight & Norris, 1970; Wight, 1969; 1970) were originally envisaged as a language course for West Indian children, but later the emphasis was changed and it was decided that many of the language skills that could be usefully developed with West Indian children would also be beneficial to a good number of native British children. The authors of the material maintained that the language of West Indian children (and, presumably, working class white children) was perfectly logical and regular and that attempts to teach the standard should be reserved for children's writing and not their speech. However, they did feel that non-standard speakers needed to develop a whole range of verbal strategies which would enable them to take part more successfully in the education process. This stance has since been criticized (cf. Sutcliffe, 1978; V. Edwards, 1979) on the grounds that the strategies which the materials were designed to remedy can in fact be found in the language which children use in non-school settings, and that the most plausible explanation for children's avoidance of particular verbal strategies in the classroom – if indeed this is the case – would seem to be in terms of situational constraints rather than an inability to do so.

The underachievement of West Indian children, first officially recognized with the publication of the DES *Statistics of Education* for 1970, was a major concern throughout the decade (Townsend, 1971, HMSO, 1977; CRC, 1977; A. Rampton, 1981). A particular bone of contention in the early 1970s was the question of the assessment of the ability of West Indian pupils. Although intelligence tests were waived in the case of non-English speaking pupils, they were a normal part of the evaluation of West Indian children until 1974, despite strong evidence that intelligence tests have little validity because of their cultural and linguistic bias (Haynes, 1971). The possibility that language played a part in the underperformance of West Indian children was finally acknowledged in 1973 with the publication of the Select Committee on Race Relations and Immigration report on Education:

> More familiarity with the problems of West Indian children has shown that many of them also need special attention in the teaching of English.... There is little doubt that neglect of special attention in the past has handicapped many children. It may partly account for the disproportionately large numbers of West Indian children in ESN schools in London... and for the generally lower standards of achievement of West

Indian pupils in some schools. It is not, of course, the only reason, but it is one which is now recognised and can be dealt with (HMSO, 1973: 13).

Following the report, a DES memorandum to Chief Education Officers on 1st November 1973 drew attention to the fact that West Indian children as well as non-English speakers may have language difficulties. The only recommendation made by the Select Committee as to how the problem could be 'dealt with', however, was that LEAs should consider how best 'with tact and discretion' they could convince West Indian parents that some of their children might need special English teaching. The Bullock Report (1975) offers only slightly more guidance. It stresses the need for a positive attitude towards the language and culture of West Indian children, which should be encouraged by initial and in-service training. It also suggests that work relating both to dialect and to improving the ability to use standard English should be encouraged on a much larger scale. Yet it gives no indication of the most suitable materials and approach for this task. Nor does it set out criteria for selecting those children in need of special teaching and it ignores the possible resistance which British-born children and their parents might offer.

Many of the difficulties in formulating a coherent policy on the language needs of children of West Indian origin can be traced to the extensive delays in recognizing their special situation within the British education system. Although some West Indian children continue even today to show the influence of Creole in their most formal speech, reading and writing (cf. V. Edwards, 1981), by the mid 1970s the majority had been born in Britain and could produce speech indistinguishable or at least close to the local white norm. The CRC (1976: 5) sums up the situation thus:

> It is ironical that at a time when Creole dialect did cause problems of communication and comprehension in schools, the question was ignored. However, by the time Creole had been identified as an educational issue, the majority of West Indian children were no longer speaking it in schools. It is often pointed out to us that some time during the early years at secondary school many West Indian pupils who up till then have used the language of the neighbourhood, begin to use Creole dialect. But its use is a deliberately social and psychological protest, an assertion of identity, not a language teaching problem.

Current practice would still seem to be little influenced by a coherent language policy. Little & Willey's (1981) survey of 70 LEAs shows that no more than a handful have made serious attempts to evaluate the needs of West Indian pupils. They point to the importance of clarifying the extent to which and the ways in which these children have 'special' language needs, and of providing guidance and support to teachers. The Rampton Report (1981) on *West Indian Children in Our Schools* goes at least some of the way towards clarifying these needs. It stresses the importance of promoting positive teacher attitudes towards the language of West Indian children through initial and in-service training. It also follows the ILEA policy statement of 1977 in encouraging schools to give West Indian pupils every opportunity to make full use of their linguistic repertoire through creative work in English, drama and discussion. It recognizes the possible ambivalence of West Indian parents to the use of an essentially low status language variety in the classroom, but argues that imaginative and creative use of a child's home language assists in developing awareness of different forms of language—including standard English—and their appropriateness for different situations.

Such an approach is radical and represents a significant departure from the practices of the 1960s and the greater part of the 1970s. Inevitably, it has attracted vituperative comment. The ILEA statement encouraging the use of Creole in poetry and drama drove one head teacher to announce that he would allow Creole in his school only 'over his dead body' (*Sunday Times,* 16 October, 1977). It remains to be seen whether this head teacher and many of his conservative colleagues in the teaching profession will be persuaded of the wisdom of this current policy lead, or resist it to the end.

Summary

The language of West Indian migrants differed in many important respects from both standard and British dialects of English. Yet for many years the rule-governed and systematic nature of these differences was overlooked by many schools and teachers, who seemed to think that West Indians simply spoke 'bad' or 'broken' English. Reports as to the continuing influence of 'patois' or 'Creole' on the children and grandchildren of the original settlers are conflicting, but there are strong indications that it remains an important social and linguistic force for many British Black people. Adaptations and developments of Creole in Britain remain to be studied in depth. It is essential, however, that those involved in the education of Black children should understand the patterns of language use in the British Black community and the symbolic role which Creole continues to play.

5 Linguistic diversity and British dialects

Linguistic diversity is thought of most often in terms of ethnic minority children in inner city schools or children in Welsh and Gaelic areas of Wales and Scotland. Such a narrow view does no justice to the considerable range of dialects spoken by working class communities all over Britain. The Rosen & Burgess (1980) survey, *Languages and Dialects of London School Children,* for instance, asked teachers to subdivide speakers of British dialects into one of three categories: London, non-London regional or standard. Seventy nine per cent of the children in the sample were classified as speakers of a non-standard dialect of English and, between them, they spoke 20 different British dialects. The London sample, as we saw in Chapter Two, was extremely cosmopolitan and included many children for whom English was a second language. It is thus quite possible that the proportion of non-standard dialect speakers would be even higher in many provincial towns and rural areas.

Most discussions of dialects return sooner or later to a comparison with standard English. For a good number of people it is possible to equate the standard with 'good' or 'correct' English while deviations from the standard are felt, at best, to be 'quaint' and, at worst, 'bad', 'sloppy' or 'incorrect'. Yet from a purely linguistic standpoint, standard English is a dialect the same as any other. Its present form is a development of the 'East Midlands' dialect spoken by Chaucer. The East Midlands included London: it was the seat of government and the power base of England. Caxton also spoke this dialect and tended to use it in preference to other English dialects, so that printing proved a powerful force in its success. It is a very salutory exercise, however, to ponder on the notion that, had the Vikings been more tenacious, York might well have been the centre of government, and the dialect of this city might now be considered standard English.

A further misconception concerns the widespread assumption that 'dialect' is spoken in rural rather than urban areas. Thus it is acceptable to talk about 'the Yorkshire dialect' or 'the Norfolk dialect', but people in Manchester and Wolverhampton simply speak bad English. Yet speakers in urban settings conform to the rules of their own dialects in the same way as Norfolk or Yorkshire or standard speakers.

There is also a feeling that a particular variety has to be quite distinct to be called a dialect. On this count, people in the Berkshire town of Reading, for instance, would not qualify as dialect speakers since features such as multiple negation *(I never asked nobody)* are found all over the country; features like *I sees* for *I see* are common in many parts of the south-west; and features such as the pronunciation of *nuffink* for *nothing* are found throughout the south-east. Language and people, however, are seldom restricted to one sphere of influence. Berkshire stands on an important dividing line between the south-west and the south-east and has many links with both regions. The fact that Reading speech is an amalgam of influences rather than completely autonomous in no way detracts from the validity of talking in terms of 'the Reading dialect'.

It is helpful at this point to distinguish between *dialect* and *accent*. Accent refers only to pronunciation while dialect includes both grammar and pronunciation. It is thus common for an educated Welshman or a Geordie to speak standard English with a regional accent, though the accent most usually associated with the standard is something known variously as 'Received Pronunciation' (RP), Oxford English, Queen's English and BBC English. Unlike all other British accents it is a social accent which does not allow the listener to locate the speaker geographically.

A wide range of literature exists on British dialects though the geographical distribution of this research is extremely uneven (see Edwards & Weltens, in press, for a review of this area). Areas like Scotland and parts of Northern England have been relatively well documented while regions like East Anglia and Wales have received very little attention. It would seem, however, that in recent times, dialect diversity is reducing. *The Survey of English Dialects* (Orton et al., 1962-71), for instance, first undertaken in the 1950's, shows many words and some grammatical features which have now completely disappeared or are only to be found in older speakers. Yet this does not mean that standard English will one day replace all other British dialects. Although vocabulary is possibly less regionally diverse now than 50 years ago, accent remains as distinct as ever and many aspects of grammar still resolutely serve to mark off standard from non-standard dialects.

How different is different?
Many teachers feel that because they have no background in

linguistics they cannot possibly be expected to discriminate between dialect features and genuine mistakes in children's work. Yet the differences between standard English and dialects are restricted to a relatively small number of areas which can be readily identified with just a little practice. The examples listed below are based on schema used by Cheshire (1982a) in her discussion of 'Dialect Features and Linguistic Conflict in School' and by Hughes & Trudgill (1979) in *English Accents and Dialects*. They are by no means intended to be an exhaustive list of differences. They are, however, amongst the most frequently occurring departures from standard English and, although they are perfectly regular dialect forms, are usually dismissed as careless mistakes by teachers. These examples can be used as a checklist to identify the main areas of difference in the dialect of a particular area, an exercise which can very usefully be undertaken with the help of the children themselves.

Main areas of difference between Standard English and British dialects

1. Verbs
   a. *Present tense verbs* sometimes differ from the standard.
      e.g. Reading dialect: I goes, you goes, he goes, we goes, they goes

      Norwich dialect: I go, you go, he go, we go, they go
   b. *Past tense words*
      - *was* used with all subjects
        e.g. I was, you was, he was, we was, they was
      - *weren't* sometimes used with *I* and *he*
        e.g. I weren't going there, he weren't at home
      - some verbs are 'regularised'
        e.g. gived, blowed, drawed, runned, fighted
      - some verbs have the same form for past participle and past tense
        e.g. *come:* I come here yesterday
             done: I done it
             went: when we'd went out we saw what had happened
             forgot: I've been and forgot it again
             took: he's took my mackintosh
      - some verbs have the same present tense and past tense form
        e.g. *see:* we see him up there yesterday
             give: I give him it last week
      - irregular past participles
        e.g. *driv:* I've driv that car up here
             writ: I've writ him a letter

  – irregular present participles
    e.g. *sat:* my mate was sat in the back laughing
    stood: he was stood watching this bloke
  c. *Modal verbs (e.g. can, may, might, will* etc. which can precede another verb as in *can go, might see)* sometimes differ from the standard
    e.g. Newcastle dialect: I don't need go
        West Yorkshire dialect: I oughtn't to say that
        Norwich dialect: they used to had

2. Negation
  a. Multiple negation is generally the rule in British dialects
    e.g. I don't want nothing
        he can't see nobody
  b. ain't (sometimes pronounced 'ent' or 'int')
    – as *be and not*
    e.g. I aint going out
        it ain't working
    – as *have and not*
    e.g. I ain't got none
  c. 'never' as past tense negative
    e.g. I never done it, it was him
  d. negation formed with 'no' or 'nae'
    e.g. he's no coming
        I've nae got it

3. Relative Pronouns
  Relative pronouns *who* (for humans) *which* (for non-humans); *that* (for both) are found in dialects, as too, are a number of other forms
    e.g. he is the man *what* said it
        he is the man *which* said it
        he is the man *as* said it
        he is the man *at* said it
    The relative pronoun can also be omitted
    e.g. he is the man said it

4. Pronouns
  a. Personal pronouns occasionally differ
    e.g. Belfast dialect: youse for you (plural)
  b. Reflexive pronouns: forms such as *hisself, theirselves* are sometimes to be heard

5. Demonstratives
  Them and *they* often correspond to standard English *those*
  e.g. I know what them students got up to

6. Prepositions
   Use of prepositions frequently differs
   e.g. *up, down, over, round,* can sometimes occur without *to* or *at*
   I went up London
   I went round my friend's house

7. Nouns of measurement
   Very often there is no plural marking
   e.g. thirteen mile, five pound

8. Adverbs
   Adverbs sometimes have the same form as adjectives
   e.g. he writes really quick
        I can't read that good

9. Comparatives and superlatives
   Many dialects allow both more/most and er/est simultaneously
   e.g. He's more taller than his brother
        She's the most beautifulest person I know

Linguistic variation

We all vary the way we speak according to the situation in which we find ourselves. Changes in speech can indicate a whole range of nuances, from respect to insolence and distance to intimacy. The varieties of language which we all command can best be described on a scale from formal to informal. Formality is difficult to define but depends on a number of different variables, including situation (where does the conversation take place – in an interview or in a pub?); topic (are you talking about nuclear physics or the price of eggs?); role relationships (is it a conversation between colleagues in the staffroom or between teacher and children in the classroom?); the sex of the speakers; and the age and age differences of the speakers.

Standard English speakers indicate differing degrees of formality in a process of 'style shifting' which is marked by subtle changes in pronunciation (e.g. *-in* for *-ing* in words like *walking* and *running*); in vocabulary (*bloke* for *man*, or *fleapit* for *cinema*); and in grammar (*We decided to finish* for *It was decided that we should finish*). This kind of sensitivity to situation is sometimes felt to be characteristic of 'educated' standard speech. Bilingual and bidialectal speakers, however, show a similar degree of accommodation. In a multilingual society differences in formality can be conveyed by language switching. Whiteley (1971), for instance, describes a housing estate in Kampala where speakers show that they are educated and economically 'comfortable' by using English, but switch to Swahili if they want to indicate feelings of brotherhood, and to Luganda in order to show deference to Ganda neighbours.

Non-standard English speakers can achieve a similar effect by varying the proportion of dialect features. Cheshire's (1982b) survey of the Reading dialect is particularly interesting in this respect. Her sample is composed of working class adolescents whose speech contains many non-standard features. As standard speakers we tend to perceive only departures from the standard in the speech of dialect speakers and the variation of non-standard features with formality goes unnoticed. There is nothing to suggest, however, that the adolescents in the Reading study are any less sensitive to differences in formality than standard speakers. Take, for instance, the following analysis of forms like *I sees* in the speech of children outside school in peer group conversation and in school in the presence of a teacher.

Figure 1: *Incidence of non-standard -s in the speech of boys and girls inside and outside school.*

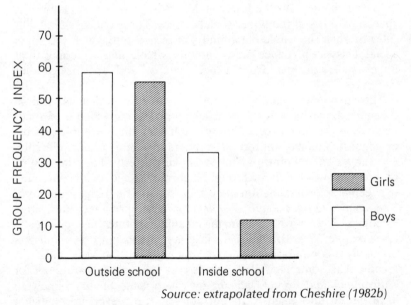

Source: extrapolated from Cheshire (1982b)

Thus, although the boys show a greater preference for non-standard forms, both boys and girls show a definite shift towards the standard in the more formal school setting. Evidence from this study and various other surveys of urban dialects (e.g. Trudgill, 1974;

Knowles, 1974) can leave us in no doubt that all speakers have a wide variety of styles at their disposal and show considerable sensitivity in their choice of language.

Notions of correctness

It is possible to locate and quantify the linguistic variation which occurs between different social groups in different situations. The example of Reading girls and boys above also draws attention to differences between male and female speech. There is certainly a considerable body of evidence (cf. Labov, 1966; Trudgill, 1974) which suggests that women tend to be extremely sensitive to prestige forms and notions of correctness and are usually in the vanguard of linguistic change. This is particularly true of lower middle class women. They belong to the most socially mobile group and their newly acquired social status is frequently mirrored by changes in their linguistic behaviour. The same applies, of course, to lower middle class men, though their linguistic adaptation seems to be less marked than that of women of the same social class. One model of language change sees the lower middle class as striving to adopt the speech patterns of the upper social classes. These changes gradually filter through the whole community, in response to which the upper social classes introduce new variants which mark them out as linguistically distinct from other groups, and so the process continues.

This dynamic quality of language is one which is seldom recognized, particularly by the teaching profession which sometimes behaves as if it had a vested interest in halting the inevitable process of linguistic change. All too often letters to *The Times* or television programmes like 'Points of View' complain bitterly about the decline of the language, either through incorrect usage or through the unacceptable pronunciation of certain words. The 'Lingo' column of *The Times Educational Supplement* also provides interesting examples of words whose changing meanings irritate the linguistically conservative. W.S. Brownlie, for instance, points out that *major* was originally a comparative adjective which meant that something was greater than something else. This is certainly an accurate gloss for Latin *major* and French *majeur*, by which route *major* is likely to have passed into English. Its current sense, however, is somewhat different, and when we speak of 'a major step' or 'a major impact' we are clearly referring to something important rather than something which is greater than something else. Language is always changing. We are, therefore, forced to the same conclusion as Brownlie: 'There is no hope of restoring "major" to its real status, so let us not waste time and tears on trying'. There will always be some doubt as the to the 'real status' of a word. It is possible, for instance, that the Indo-European root from which Latin *'major'* is derived meant something quite different.

A possibly more striking example is the recent development of 'gay' as a non-pejorative term of reference for a homosexual. This meaning of 'gay' has gained considerable currency in the last few years, to the extent that many people deliberately avoid using it in the former sense of 'joyful' or 'happy'. We clearly have no right to assume that any particular state gives us the true meaning of any word. English is a living and constantly developing language.

Much of the controversy about which forms are acceptable derives from the fact that writing is more conservative than speech. Norms for writing lag behind speech by a generation or more though this in no way implies that writing is not subject to the same pressure for change. A rapid survey of English literature from Kingsley Amis to Jane Austen to Shakespeare to Chaucer can leave us in no doubt as to the nature of language change. The differing rates of change for speech, and writing do, however, generate certain tensions, but attempts to prescribe what is correct at any given time are doomed to failure. The examples below, taken from Mittins et al. (1970), should make this clear.

	Formal		*Informal*	
	Speech	*Writing*	*Speech*	*Writing*
He did not do *as* well *as* the experts had predicted				
The data *is* sufficient for our purposes				
The performance ended early *due to* illness among the players				
Competitors should try *and* arrive in good time				
We *have got* to finish the job				
The instruments were *pretty* reliable				

A number of things may strike you as you decide which of these examples you might use in which situations. Almost certainly you will find that you would use the smallest number of examples in formal writing and the largest in informal speech, patterns of usage for formal speech and informal writing falling between these two poles.

You will probably have no difficulty in deciding what is wrong with some of the sentences, but will be at a loss to know what is unacceptable about others, though all were considered examples of 'bad English' in the not too distant past. Most importantly, even if you have no difficulty in deciding for yourself where you could or could not use a particular form, the dangers of prescriptivism will soon become apparent if you compare your answers with those of your friends. There is a wide range of variation in what is acceptable to different speakers even when they come from similar educational and social backgrounds. It is obviously not always possible to say what is and what is not acceptable in language. There is a central core on which we are unanimous, but there are many hazy areas around the edges about which there is considerable disagreement. These edges are a reminder of the dynamic nature of language and examples of language change in progress.

Our preoccupation with minutiae, however, tends to make us lose sight of the fact that all language – and not simply standard English – can be seen as a highly structured, highly productive, rule-governed activity. In view of the flexibility of language and the extreme sensitivity to situation which all speakers show, arguments about 'good' and 'bad' English must be seen in the context of social judgements and not linguistic ones.

Attitudes towards language

From a purely linguistic point of view, there is no evidence to challenge the notion that all languages and dialects are equal. It is possible to hold up examples of some vocabulary or structures in one language or dialect as arguably superior to those of another. Some people might claim, for instance, that English is more precise than French because it makes a distinction between the progressive (*I am talking now*) and the habitual (*I talk all the time*). It is equally possible, however, to find counter examples in the other language or dialect. Thus, French has the subjunctive mood which makes it possible to distinguish between *je sais qu'il vient* (I know he's coming) and *je ne crois pas qu'il vienne* (I don't think he's coming). In the final analysis, all such advantages and disadvantages cancel one another out and it is a completely pointless exercise to try and establish the superiority of one language or dialect over another.

But whereas no one variety is superior from a linguistic point of view, there can be no doubt that some language varieties are socially superior to others. One of the pioneering techniques in the investigation of attitudes towards language has been the 'matched guise technique' (Lambert et al., 1960). 'Judges' listen to a number of recordings but, unknown to them, one speaker is heard twice, once using the non-standard dialect or minority language, and once using the standard variety. Work which has been done on British dialects using this technique (see, for example, Giles & Powesland, 1975) shows a hierarchy of preferences in which highest status is assigned to standard speech, followed by rural dialects and finally urban dialects. RP speakers are seen as more intelligent and competent than speakers of regional dialects, though non-standard and non-RP speaking judges do tend to evaluate regionally accented speech as marking a greater sense of integrity and being more socially attractive.

Many people react on an emotional level to evidence that no one variety is inherently superior. In spite of an intellectual grasp of the implications of such evidence, they have a gut feeling that one accent or dialect is intrinsically more beautiful than another. This recurring theme in discussions of linguistic superiority has led to the formulation of two competing hypotheses – the 'inherent value' hypothesis which holds that there is something intrinsic to certain accents which makes them more pleasant than others, and the 'imposed norm' hypothesis which states that the high status and accepted pleasantness of certain accents are merely reflections of the status of their speakers. It is possible to test these hypotheses by asking 'judges' totally unfamiliar with a language to evaluate different dialects of that language. If high status is attributable to some intrinsic quality, this will be recognized by native speaker and foreign judge alike. Various experiments have been carried out on different dialects of French and Greek (Giles et al., 1974; Giles et al., 1975) using English speakers, and the results suggest that there is nothing inherent in certain varieties which makes them more attractive than others.

It is interesting to interpret reactions to British dialects in the light of these findings. There is, for instance, a widespread preference for rural dialects over urban dialects so that whereas Highland Scots or Somerset are generally felt to be pleasing and attractive, Cockney or Birmingham dialects are almost always considered ugly and jarring. This pattern of preference seems to reflect our nostalgic attachment to the countryside and dislike of everything associated with city life. It is certainly interesting to note that when recordings of British dialects are played to English speakers from other parts of the world there seems to be a marginal preference for urban dialects (Trudgill, 1982). This might well be because non-natives are more familiar with urban British speech.

English as a mother tongue: policy and practice in British schools
All the arguments put forward in this chapter have suggested that, although non-standard dialects may deviate from standard English, their speakers are conforming to perfectly logical and consistent rules of grammar in the same way as standard speakers. It has been suggested that we are dealing with linguistic difference rather than deficit and that the low status of non-standard speech should be explained in terms of negative attitudes on the part of standard speakers rather than inherent inferiority in the non-standard. This is not an altogether new interpretation of events. Hollingworth (1977), reports the lively correspondence which took place in *The Rochdale Observer* during the 1890s around a certain school inspector's suggestion that dialect should be incorporated into the curriculum. 'Lancashire', for instance, had this to say:

> Is it worth while causing the child to leave the speech entirely in which he can express himself most forcibly? What is language for? To express our thoughts, and the more expressive we can make that expression the better for us and our hearers. Yet [certain people] would practically take away from the child the ability to express himself in the most natural manner, for they would say to the teacher 'reduce the child's vocabulary'- make him write and speak only in a language fixed by southern writers and speakers who know nothing of his ideas, of his modes of expression, of the beauties of his everyday speech, and when you have done all of that to the child, when you have given him only an artificial method of conveying his thoughts to others, say that you have done your duty to the child, that you have driven him from a dialect which abounds in vulgarities and expressions of bad breeding.

In the context of a crusade to educate the masses which had barely been in progress 20 years at the time of this correspondence it is not surprising that arguments like those of 'Lancashire' were largely overlooked by teachers who must have strongly associated dialect with the language of ignorance. The debate on the adequacy of non-standard English has thus continued over the decades. The Newbolt Report of 1921 on the Teaching of English in England had no doubt, for instance, that:

> It is emphatically the business of the Elementary School to teach all its pupils who either speak a definite dialect or whose speech is disfigured by vulgarisms, to speak standard English, and to speak it clearly, and with expression. (p.65)

The Spens Report of 1939 on Secondary Education refers in a similar vein to the 'slovenly, ungrammatical and often incomprehensible' nature of the 'English of common usage'. The general consensus, then, for a considerable period of time was that dialect speech was educationally unacceptable and that teachers' main weapons of attack should be grammatical drills and parsing. By the 1960s, however, an important distinction had been made between descriptive and prescriptive approaches to English and the usefulness of grammatical exercises was being called into question (cf. Plowden, 1967). There was also a growing concern about the relationship between school language, working class language and educational failure (cf. for instance, the Newsom Report, HMSO, 1963).

Bernstein's theory of language codes

The work of Basil Bernstein (see, for instance, *Class Codes and Control,* vol. 1) proved particularly influential in this debate, providing a veneer of academic respectability to prejudices about the inadequacy of non-standard English and the linguistic shortcomings of dialect speakers. Bernstein polarized the 'elaborated' and 'restricted' codes as two ideal types. They differ in grammar and vocabulary, the restricted code exploiting a much narrower range of possibilities. It is held to use, for example, fewer complex clauses and verbal groups and a smaller number of nouns, adjectives, verbs and adverbs. It has more sociocentric sequences like 'you know' and 'isn't it' and shows fewer grammatical changes in the switch from descriptive and narrative speech to explanations. The restricted code makes use of extra-verbal channels whereas the main function of the elaborated code is to put over relatively explicit meaning verbally. The elaborated code thus gives access to 'universalistic' orders of meaning which are less context bound, while the restricted code gives access to 'particularistic' orders of meaning which are more context bound.

Bernstein attributes the development of the two codes to different patterns of socialization and considers that if children are able to use only the restricted code the processes and content of perception, thinking, remembering and learning will be adversely affected. The appeal of this theory of language codes is easy to understand since it appears to provide an explanation for why some children do better than others in school. Any child who does not have access to the elaborated code, for instance, will be at a disadvantage in an educational system concerned with making explicit and elaborating principles and operations through language. Such a child's grammar and lexis will lack 'the hierarchical and flexible structure and range of units for the encoding and decoding of messages' as well as 'the referential anchorage to non-linguistic events'.

Bernstein's work has, however, attracted bitter criticism from a wide range of writers (see Stubbs, 1976, and J. Edwards, 1979b, for the fullest discussion of this area). It has been argued, for instance, that his theory of language codes is both untestable and unrelated to linguistic evidence (Jackson, 1974). The lack of linguistic evidence is a theme pursued further by writers such as Labov (1969), Trudgill (1975) and Stubbs (1976), and it is certainly striking that the brief examples of speech which appear in Bernstein's work tend to be either invented or based on artificial test situations. For example, one of his studies was on the differences between groups of public school boys and day release students who were asked in the presence of an interviewer to discuss capital punishment. The possibility that situational factors may have inhibited the working class boys is not discussed.

Yet other writers have demonstrated convincingly the dramatic effect which situation can have on a speaker. Labov (1969) for instance, describes two interviews with Leon, an 8 year old Harlem boy. In the first interview very little progress is made and Leon gives short, non-committal responses to the questions put to him. In the second meeting, however, his best friend is invited to come along, everybody (including the interviewer) sits down on the floor, food is passed around and taboo subjects are introduced into the conversation. The social distance between interviewer and child has been reduced and Leon shows himself to be a normal 8 year old who speaks fluently and intelligently.

Another consideration which needs to be taken into account in any attempt to evaluate the work of Bernstein is the way in which his views have modified dramatically over the years. In early papers it is easy to get the impression that the elaborated code can be equated with middle class speech and the restricted code with working class speech. His work is permeated with value judgements – the very choice of 'restricted' and 'elaborated' is unfortunate – and he sometimes makes sweeping and unsubstantiated statements. In later papers his expression is far less powerful. He states explicitly that the working class child is not linguistically deprived and that there may be a case for the teacher to attempt to understand the child's dialect rather than deliberately trying to change it.

Wider repercussions of Bernstein's work

The fact remains, however, that Bernstein's work, and particularly the earlier papers, have been extremely influential on both sides of the Atlantic. In America in the 1960s, for instance, there was a tremendous proliferation of compensatory education programmes for children described variously as 'socially disadvantaged' and 'linguistically' or 'culturally deprived'. Some of these programmes openly acknowledge their debt to Bernstein:

> Our estimation of the language of the culturally deprived agrees with that of Bernstein, who maintains that this language is not merely an undeveloped version of standard English, but is a basically non-logical mode of expressive behaviour which lacks the formal properties for the organisation of thought. (Bereiter et al., 1966)

Not all characterizations of non-standard speech as inadequate or inferior are associated so openly with Bernstein. Indeed, close scrutiny of his work would provide very little justification for such bold statements. Nonetheless, his work on language and class has loaned an air of respectability to discussions such as these. Significantly, the same weaknesses noted by critics of Bernstein's work also appear in other treatments of verbal deprivation. Situational constraints are frequently overlooked and there is a widespread assumption that working class parents simply do not speak to their children either often enough or in the right way. This is reflected for instance in the Bullock Report, *A Language for Life,* which advocates that health visitors should urge parents to 'bathe children in language'. Herbstein (1980) describes a project in the Ladywood area of Birmingham involving health visitors, speech therapists and social workers where contact is made with mothers in supermarkets and children are distributed with 'Mum, talk to me' stickers. The rationale for this scheme is that 'inner city children are simply not being spoken to enough by their parents in their vital early years'.

It is interesting to speculate how much conclusions such as these are based on casual rather than careful observation. Equally important is the need to guard against the ethnocentric and middle class bias in what we do observe. We tend to assume that there is only one acceptable model for language learning. Cross-cultural study, however, shows that there are many possibilities (cf. Saville-Troike, 1982). Talbert's (1969) study of black families in St Louis is particularly interesting in this respect. Her observations confirmed that there is relatively little verbal interaction between parents and children, but she points out that:

> The child was privy to the continual exchange of information between adults concerning problems, aspirations and often feelings and comments about the child himself. The child is learning then not by direct and elaborate explanations but rather by exposure, listening and peer group interaction.

A key factor in understanding the widespread attention which the work of Bernstein, and theories of verbal deprivation in general, have received is the link which they make between linguistic and cognitive deficiency. The processes of language are directly observable whereas those of cognition are not. This, presumably, is what makes the linking of the two an attractive proposition, but it is important to remember that no clear relationship has ever been demonstrated. Discussions of language and cognition make frequent reference, for instance, to abstract thought, though nobody has actually made clear what constitutes the abstract thought of which non-standard speakers are allegedly incapable. As Houston (1969) remarks:

> Abstract thinking is sometimes said to consist of the ability to generalize and categorize. Presumably, grammatical utterances could not be constructed at all without the internalized notions of grammatical category, and novel utterances could not be formed without generalization from previously experienced patterns.

Todd (1974) also identifies a flaw in the logic of the cognitive deficiency argument when he points out that all varieties of English have been used successfully in teaching Christian doctrine which contains concepts as abstract as 'grace', 'redemption', 'transubstantiation' and 'three divine persons in one God'. It is not surprising that the achievements of American compensatory education programmes have, by and large, been a great disappointment to the interventionists: they were designed to remedy linguistic and cognitive deficiencies which have not been shown to exist. Efforts in this direction in a British setting can hardly be expected to be any more successful.

Reactions against the notion of verbal deprivation in English teaching

By the mid 1970s, a counterforce to the theories of linguistic deprivation was emerging. It was clearly embodied, for example, in the Nuffield Programme on Linguistics in Language Teaching established in 1964 under the auspices of the Schools Council, which led to the publication of *Language in Use*, lesson plans designed to increase children's understanding of the nature and function of language (Doughty et al., 1971). It was also the keynote of the 1975 Bullock Report, *A Language for Life*, which made strong pleas for schools to respect the linguistic and cultural diversity of their pupils:

> No child should be expected to cast off the language and culture of the home as he crosses the school threshold and the curriculum should reflect those aspects of his life. (p.543)

The presence of ethnic minority children in British schools has also contributed to important modifications in approaches to language teaching. There has been a growing awareness, for instance, of the educational potential of linguistic diversity and an exploration of how children's language - including working class children's non-standard dialects—can be exploited in a classroom setting. Rosen & Burgess (1980) report a number of important initiatives in this area. The interest stimulated by their survey, *Languages and Dialects of London School Children,* led to the setting up of a working party on curriculum materials for the study of linguistic diversity. This diversity was conceived in multidimensional terms:

> It can mean, for instance, varieties of English: dialects, group languages, slangs and jargons and styles, private language, anti-languages, non-verbal languages, as well as the languages associated with sex and age and class and occupation. (p.120)

Teachers involved in the working group have collaborated to produce a booklet called *The Languages Book.* Published by the ILEA English Centre, this is an excellent workbook for the secondary age range which covers topics such as different languages and dialects, learning to speak, how English has changed and what other people think about the way you speak. Other writers have also realized the potential of linguistic diversity as a classroom resource and materials currently available for secondary pupils include Michael Newby's *Making Language* books (OUP, 1981) and Moira Healy's *Your Language* books (OUP, 1981). Ruth Cole and John Wyatt's *Keeping in Touch* (Macmillan, 1981) is aimed primarily at students on vocational courses, while the linguistic awareness of younger pupils is the focus for Frank McNeil and Neil Mercer's *Primary Language Project* (A. & C. Black, 1982). Two of the programmes on the videocassette for teachers in the ILEA Learning Service Materials' *Language in the Multiethnic Primary School* can also be mentioned conveniently at this point: 'Listen to us' deals with linguistic and cultural diversity while 'The way we speak' considers dialect and learning.

The underlying rationale for the development of curriculum materials such as these is very adequately summed up by Rosen & Burgess:

> Children who are to develop as successful, confident users of language have to be encouraged to look beyond habits and prejudices ... to the nature and implications of judgements about 'good' and 'bad' language. Children need to be aware of the ways in which language can exert power or confirm weakness. By exploring the functions and effects, as well as the

constraints, of forms of spoken and written language, children may be enabled to revalue their own skills, gain much needed confidence through an appreciation of their ability to make sense of language in different modes, to move between dialects, styles, accents themselves and to interpret intention and motive from the language they attend to in others. (p. 121)

Awareness of the importance of language and a distrust of traditional prescriptivism have thus grown considerably throughout the 1970s, and have also been reflected in developments such as the 'Language Across the Curriculum' movement, stimulated by the work of writers like Barnes, Britton & Rosen (1969) and Barnes (1976). There is a strong suggestion that all teachers and not simply language teachers should be involved in language teaching and a focus on the ways that language can both obscure and help the learning process. This atmosphere of linguistic awareness has had a number of important educational repercussions. There is an increasing appreciation, for instance, of the common language needs of all children irrespective of their backgrounds. But whereas in the 1960s and early 1970s discussion centred on the linguistic deficiencies of non-English and dialect speaking children, there is now more open recognition of the validity of dialect and the advantages of bilingualism, and initiatives which bring children's language into the classroom are multiplying at an impressive rate (cf. V. Edwards, 1979; Levine, 1982). There is also a growing understanding of the benefits of including second language learners wherever possible in mainstream classes rather than isolating them in special classes and centres.

Important strides have been made, too, in identifying language issues which demand consistent treatment throughout the child's career, such as limited intervention in children's oral reading (Moon & Raban, 1980); the counterproductive nature of correcting dialect features (Edwards, op. cit., Richmond, 1979; A. Rampton, 1981) and the importance of creating situations where the use of dialect is valued (Rampton, op. cit.). These remain to be translated into policy at school level and will form the focus of the remaining chapters of this book.

Summary

The nature of dialect difference is often misunderstood. Departures from standard English tend to be dismissed as 'wrong' or 'careless' and the systematic, rule-governed nature of dialects is generally overlooked. A causative relationship between language and educational success has been postulated, though never actually proved. Far less attention, however, has been paid to the role which attitudes towards language differences may be playing in under-performance. Nonetheless there has been a definite move away in recent years from linguistic prescriptivism. The presence of ethnic and linguistic minority children in schools has stimulated renewed interest in the situation of British dialect speakers and there is a growing appreciation of the value of building on, rather than downgrading, children's existing linguistic repertoires and sensitivity to language.

6 Children talking

It is not insignificant that the traditional curriculum concentrated on the three R's to the exclusion of children talking. Indeed large classes often demanded management strategies specifically designed to prevent children talking. Teachers today work under more favourable conditions and usually have more enlightened attitudes towards talk in the classroom. There have been significant developments in our understanding of the function of children's talk, particularly in the last ten years. The Bullock Report (1975), for instance, examines the relationship of language to thinking and learning (Chapter 4) and discusses the develpment of children's talking and listening skills in school (Chapter 10). The work of Douglas Barnes, particularly *From Communication to Curriculum,* has been very influential in support of the argument that people learn more from talking than from listening. Connie and Harold Rosen's *The Language of Primary School Children* has made an equally important impact in advocating that language should be treated as something which permeates the curriculum rather than as an isolated activity. Talk has finally achieved educational respectability.

Talking with younger children

Yet in many classes teachers monopolize the talk (cf. Stubbs, 1976, Chapter 6). Children respond rather than initiate and seldom have the opportunity to do more than give summary replies to teacher questions. It would seem that this is a pattern which begins in the nursery and continues throughout a child's school life. Wood et al. (1980) describe how nursery teachers and playgroup leaders taking part in a project undertaken by the Oxford Pre-School Research Group made half hour recordings of a part of their day which they considered typical. An analysis of the tapes showed that the 'rapport dimension', whereby the adult acknowledges or repeats what the child has said, is high:

Child: I'm going to play with cars
Adult: Oh lovely!

Child: And I…I'm going to do my painting
Adult: Super!

So, too, was the 'management talk' in which adults organize children:

Janet, have you had your milk dear? No, well go and get it then before it's all gone.
John, I think you'd better go and get a tissue for that nose of yours. There's one in the loo. Off you go.

There was little evidence, however, of sustained conversation of an intellectually more demanding nature. Adults tended to dominate the conversation, asking questions of a testing nature and giving children little opportunity to think and answer. This has certainly been a feature of many conversations I have recorded between young children and adults, other than their parents, assuming a didactic role. Take, for instance, the following exchanges between 5 year old Dafydd and a student teacher working in his class:

Teacher: What's this, then?
Dafydd: Conker
Teacher: Did you collect it yesterday when we went out for our nature
          walk?
Dafydd: I collected acorn in its…
Teacher: Oh, in its shell. It sits in a sort of little cup, doesn't it? Have you
          got any conkers at home?
Dafydd: Yes
Teacher: How many have you got?
Dafydd: I've got one on a string
Teacher: On a string? What do you do with that one?
Dafydd: It's…
Teacher: It's to play a game. What sort of game do you play with it?
Dafydd: You have a conker on a string and you try to smash the other
          one
Teacher: And who do you play that with?
Dafydd: Daddy
Teacher: Daddy. Ceri's too young to play I expect
Dafydd: Yes

The imbalance in talk between the professional and the child hardly supports the widely held view that, because of their special training, nursery and infant teachers are well equipped to promote language development. Such an assumption is challenged even further when it emerges that recordings of the same child with his father and then with his best friend (see V. Edwards, 1983) are not characterized by the hesitant and truncated responses of the teacher-child interaction, but show him to be a talkative and verbally adept child.

My own anecdotal observations are supported by the considerably more systematic approach of Tizard et al. (1980) on the language of 4 year old children. They found that the main differences in children's language occurred between home and school and, interestingly, that differences in language use between working class and middle class children in the home setting were very small or absent. At home conversations were frequently longer and more equally balanced between adult and child. Children asked more questions and answered adults more frequently. In view of the fact that mothers in the study played much more with their children, talked to them much more and answered many more questions than did the teachers, the researchers understandably suggest that the professional's advice on how to talk to children may often be wide of the mark:

> How and why parents talk to their children is the resultant of many complex factors, notably status relationships within the family, and also what seems important to them to communicate. This in turn is likely to depend on a whole set of attitudes, including their belief about what the children are going to need to function effectively in society. Quite aside, then, from whether it is wise to make people self-conscious about the way they talk to their children, it seems likely that intervention at this superficial level will be ineffective. (p.50).

Some teachers are, of course, significantly more successful than others in promoting productive talk with children. It would seem that an essential factor in such success is a move away from the asymmetry in relationships which characterizes much teacher-child interaction. Practitioners who do not bombard the child with questions, offering their own personal views, seem to achieve a far more active response. Wood et al. (1980: 14), for instance, offer the following as an example of a productive exchange:

Child: There's a zoo in Bristol, isn't there?
Adult: There is a zoo, yes
Child: Have you been to it?
Adult: Once a long time ago, when I was a little girl, I went to it
Child: Ohh...
Adult: Do you go to it sometimes when you go to your granny?
Child: Yes we might go. Daddy said we can go to the seaside or the...uhh...or the zoo...uhh...when we go there.
Adult: Oh, that would be lovely. Which do you think you'd rather go to?
Child: Ahmmm – the zoo?
Adult: The zoo. It's nicer than the seaside, isn't it?
Child: Hmm, I think it's nicer. No I'd like to go to the seaside first, and bring some shells – to granny and pampam, still I brought some for them last time – might bring some more.

Talking with older children

The language of classrooms at the other end of the educational scale would appear to be equally high in 'controlling moves' on the part of the teacher. Stubbs (1976), for instance, draws attention to 'chalk and talk' lessons which are characterized by 'the way the teacher constantly explains things, corrects pupils, evaluates and edits their language, summarizes the discussion and controls the direction of the lesson'. Children learn to assume a passive role, rarely initiating discussion and giving short answers to well-defined questions.

This, of course, is not inevitably a function of the teaching process. American Indians often look on speech as an unnecessary instrusion in the learning process and stress instead observation and participation. Black Americans would also seem to make greater use of observation and less use of explicit verbal explanations than is the norm for 'Anglo' education. Stubbs (op.cit.: pp.100-2) points significantly to discussion as a challenging alternative to 'chalk and talk' approaches to learning, drawing on the following example:

(A discussion about corporal punishment has been under way for about ten minutes.)

T: You don't think corporal punishment is er - in a school - you think corporal punishment is all right at home - but er not in a school.

P1:   No, I don't say that. I said until a certain level the cane I am against.

T: 'Until a certain level' - I don't understand you.

P1:   Ah yes, I explained ten minutes ago.

T: Well, I still don't - 'until a certain level', I don't - I don't quite understand what you mean.

P1:   The cane I am against, slaps I am for.

T: O yeah - I see.

P2:   I can't agree - if er a smack can do nothing.

T: A slap?

P2:   A slap can do nothing if er - I don't know - a text to learn by heart can do nothing.

T: You think that a text is just the same thing - thing to give er - something like em - lines - to write out or to learn - it's just the same thing?

P2:   It's not the same thing - I don't say that - it has no more effect.

T: It has no more effect.

(The discussion continued with P2 telling a story about a friend of a friend who had committed suicide after being corporally punished in school. The teacher brought the discussion to a close as follows.)

T: Would you like to er say - sum up what you think about corporal punishment in general?

P1:   In general?

T: Like to sum up, yeah - what you think now after this discussion - in a few words to say - what you think.

P1:   I am still of the same opinion. I am against.

T: You're against corporal punishment.

P1:   Yes.

T: And er

P1:   There are too many bad consequences in the future for -

P2:   But I keep the same opinion as the er

T: You have the same opinion.

P2:   Yes, because what you said - what you said - what you told us, it's nothing. I have destroyed - for me. I think that - it seems to me that - it seems for me that with the last example that I gave you, all your opinions are com - all your em -

T: Arguments.

P2:   Arguments are completely destroyed.

T: For you.

P2:   Yes, I think so.

T: Well, I think we'll leave it at that.

This example departs from the pattern of teacher initiation - pupil response - teacher feedback (cf. Sinclair & Coulthard, 1975) which characterizes many classroom exchanges. Instead pupils both initiate exchanges and question the interpretation of what they have said in something which approximates much more closely to what we would normally understand by discussion.

An important point which emerges from this illustration is that social and cognitive aspects of learning cannot be separated. Richardson (1982) reinforces and expands on this theme. He emphasizes that discussion exercises are not chaotic, and do not necessarily promote 'chat' as distinct from 'talk', or 'conversation' as distinct from 'debate'. Rather, they can be used to stimulate three very healthy developments: first, practice in certain linguistic and conceptual skills; second, the learning of certain social skills in their relationship with each other; third the fostering of certain moral attitudes. The first two of these developments are largely self-evident and have been widely discussed by writers such as Stanford (1969), Barnes (1976) and Bridges (1979). It is useful, however, to dwell a little on the third development and its particular relevance for culturally and linguistically diverse classrooms. As Richardson points out:

Discussion exercises simulate and stimulate moral culture by requiring participants to see both themselves and each other in a particular way: as centres of consciousness, subjects who can and do say 'I', with wishes, intentions, hopes, ideals; they are not objects to be manipulated, not empty vessels to be given 'inputs'. (This common term 'input' surely implies a terrible failure in understanding and moral respect on the part of many teachers and conference organisers). If people attend to you as someone from whom they learn, you feel valued, sure of yourself, secure. You feel that you for your part can dare to attend to others – that is, to risk being challenged and changed by them, by what they know, by how they think and see. This is important for teacher-pupil relationships, it is worth emphasizing, as well as for relationships amongst pupils. (p.109)

Discussion exercises can thus perform an extremely valuable equalizing function which can reflect the diversity present in a classroom and build upon it. On some occasions, for instance, it will be both possible and desirable for children belonging to the same cultural or ethnic group to work together, in which case it would be natural for them to use their own first language where this is not English. Such an approach regards diversity as a resource rather than a problem or a threat.

Talk and the second language learner

The very great emphasis placed on reading and writing skills in school means that the importance of talk is often overlooked. We have been arguing. however, that one of the teacher's central roles is to create an atmosphere where children can develop their communicative competence, both between pupils and between teacher and pupils. In a class which contains second language learners it is particularly important that children should be constantly exposed to language and strongly . motivated to communicate. Children are essentially pattern learners, whether in the acquisition of their mother tongue or a second language. But they operate their own rule systems, arriving only gradually at the adult model or the target language, and it is doubtful whether 'correction' is any more efficacious for the second language learner than it is for the young child. Both seem to consider it an unnecessary intrusion when they are more interested in putting across an idea than in achieving sometimes arbitrary grammatical correctness and both start using the 'correct' form spontaneously rather than in response to adult exhortations.

Children should therefore be given every opportunity to hear as wide a range of language as possible, and 'collaborative learning' techniques can clearly play an important part in this process. By encouraging children to work in pairs and groups, for instance, the teacher is extending both the quantity and range of language to which they are exposed. Such an approach also provides realistic motivation for children to communicate with one another, so that they can test the acceptability of rules which they have formulated for themselves on the basis of the language they have heard.

Building on children's verbal skills

The school promotes a certain set of linguistic and cultural norms. When children do not conform to these norms they are very often seen as in some way deficient. It is certainly true that the language experience which these children bring to school is often very different from that of the middle class English child, but it would be wrong to assume either that it is inferior or that it has no part to play in the child's formal education. The examples which follow are valuable for a number of reasons. They acknowledge that the child has something useful and interesting to contribute to the class. Such an approach represents a sound base on which to build and a far more honest response to linguistic diversity than one which ignores, criticizes or rejects. There are also far-reaching implications for the teacher. The realization that children from other backgrounds often have access to rich and varied cultures very different from their own is likely to greatly enhance understanding and appreciation of these children and their ability to learn.

Verbal duelling

Teasing and taunting are universal childhood practices. The Opies in their classic work, *The Lore and Language of Schoolchildren,* talk of the 'armoury of ready responses' and the 'lack of inhibition' about using them which characterize many children's exchanges. They point, among other things, to the importance of the ability to have the last word:

> First boy: If I had a face like yours I'd put it on a wall and throw a brick at it.
>
> Second boy: If I had a face like *yours* I'd put it on a brick and throw a wall at it.
>
> *(Opie & Opie, 1977:65)*

Repartee of this order is a feature of the interaction of all children in all cultures. In many West Indian children, however, this is sometimes formalized into a highly developed skill. The art is to take the insult offered by your opponent and transform or better it to your advantage, or point to flaws in logic. Such insults are, of course, ritual and not genuine. They are designed to entertain and take place invariably in front of an audience of other children. They call for quick-wittedness and a high degree of skill. Take, for instance, the following exchanges between two 10 year olds recorded by Steve Hoyle in a Lambeth primary school.

Exchanges	*Commentary*
B: Right, then, look pon you eye. You haven't got pupils in you eye. You can't see. Take the shame. don't complain!	
A: I got dirt in my eye. I got dirt ina my eye, bogey nose, you. You clean out you nose ...	Transformation of eye into nose
B: You big nose. When you breath the same nose ...	Nose theme sustained
A: You stretch neck large, you! When you breathe you nose come up big as a saucer	Nose theme sustained
B: You see any puff head	Attempt to change theme
A: Just shave you teeth, shave you teeth	Successful change of theme
B: I can't shave my teeth man	Challenge of logic
A: Well cut them	Transformation of *shave* into *cut*
B: Me can't cut them	B claims victory of logic
A: You can	
B: If I cut them I have no teeth. Me have to go like this (noises) Take the shame, don't complain! Alright!	Concluding formula

It is also interesting to note that duelling skills are a highly developed part of a number of other cultures represented in British classrooms. They form an important part, for instance, in wedding celebrations as far apart as Cyprus and India. In Northern India the women on the bride's side hurl insults in song at the bridegroom and his family, while the women on the groom's side retaliate in kind. Take the popular Gujarati taunts:

Rail gaadi aavi mumbeyno maal laavi
Jowone maari baheno aa rail gaadi aavi
(The train has arrived bringing goods from Bombay
Look ladies! The train has come)

Railma bharya *chokha,* weway batha *bokha*
Jowone maari baheno aa rail gaadi aawi
(The train is full of rice and the groom's party are toothless
Look ladies! ...)

Railma bharya *ringna* weway batha *thingna*
Jowone maari baheno aa rail gaadi aawi
(The train is full of aubergines and the groom's party are all shorties
Look oh ladies! ...)

The full effect of these rhyming couplets can perhaps be better appreciated by substituting a pair of English rhyming words:

The train has come in full of rice
And the bridegroom's party are a load of mice.

The universal enjoyment of teasing and taunting behaviour of this kind can usefully be brought into play in second language learning games which involve all the children in a class. The National Association for the Teaching of English (undated) suggests two different patterns. In the first, the game is to accuse and deny, and the task is to produce a tape of accusations and denials which have to range between rudeness and politeness. Inexperienced groups could be given a starter such as:

P1 Hey you just put my pencil in your pocket.
P2 No I didn't. Who'd want that blunt old thing?

In the second pattern, the task is to produce a tape of boasts, going one better each time. Again an inexperienced group could be given a starter such as,

P1 I stayed out till 3 o'clock last night
P2 You couldn't've stayed out till 3 o'clock last night
P1 Why not?
P2 You're too scared of your Dad.

Games like these have the advantage of drawing on both native and non-native speakers, and providing useful practice for both form and function in language, as well as introducing elements of fun and fantasy.

Role play and dramatization
West Indian verbal duels usually take place between children and adolescents. Indian and Cypriot duels, on the other hand, take place between adults, not children, though children are invariably present. In all cases, however, the performance skills exemplified in the exchanges above are highly prized within the community and children are often strongly motivated to acquire such skills. Teachers can play an important part in helping children to extend and consolidate their linguistic repertoire simply by recognizing the range of skills which they bring to school. They can also build upon these skills in areas such as role play and drama. Many teachers have commented, for instance, on the performance skills of West Indian pupils and the sensitive use of both Creole and British English which emerges during role play. Several such examples are contained in *Thursday Afternoons,* poems and stories written by girls at a secondary school in Slough. Take, for instance, 'Boys, Boys, All the Time' by Paulette Christian:

Ring, ring, ring, the telephone goes. I quickly run down the stairs to answer.

P: Hello, who is it?

Q: Hi Paulette, are you going to Reading tomorrow night?

P: I don't really know. It all depends if my mum lets me go.

Q: Well ask her, and phone me if you can. (I go into the front room and ask her.)

P: Mum, can I go to Reading on Saturday?

M: Parlette, a were you say you warnt fe go?

P: Reading.

M: A who along dere?

P: There's a party down there, and my friend Glenda asked if I want to go.

M: Me know why you warnt fe go dong dere.

P: Why?

M: Becarse fu you man dong dere. You warnt fe come in de house one o'cluck and two o'cluck in de morning.

P: No I haven't got a man, I just want to enjoy myself.

M: When Boysie come me a go tell him dat you warnt to go Reading to go look man.

P: No I do not want to go Reading just to look man, and you only think of of one thing.

M: A wah me a hear Parlette, you mus a warnt me fe go tell Boysie you a tark backchat to me, and you jus warnt fe go Reading to go look man, but when you have fe you big belly you no put one foot in dis ya house. If you do, me a go trow hut warter pun you, so you just go bout ya business, and you hear wha me tell you, okay!

I shut the door and go upstairs to get dressed. I come downstairs and I go to tell my mum that I'm going. To my surprise I see my dad in the front room, and he is arguing with my mother. I open the door a little way, and my dad is saying to my mum:

D: Enid, why arl de time you jus a say Parlette a go out and go look man, you mean to say dat you no even trus Parlette? Man, she just fifteen, and you tink she a go look man at dis age lef de child man!

M: Ah right, Boysie, me a go lef she but when she come in dis house from Reading with she big belly, nar carl me name, Boysie. And Parlette, if you carl me name me a go teck up sumeting and bussit in a ya head, and police can carry me go a station, caurse whah me no care.

Paulette demonstrates an impressive control over a wide range of language, from the standard English of the narrative to the Anguillan Creole of the mother. It is very easy to assume that only older children show linguistic sensitivity on this scale. Yet, given the opportunity, younger children, too, demonstrate a surprising range of skills. Puppetry can be a very useful stimulus for allowing young children to show both their knowledge of different accents and dialects and impressive sophistication in adapting language to situation. Wiles (1981) uses an extract from a very interesting puppet play performed by second year children in Princess May Junior School, London after listening to the Caribbean Folk Tale, 'How Ackee and Saltfish became friends' (Wight et al. 1978a).

Cecil Saltfish: Please Mr Paw Paw, would you please untie me?

Paw Paw: How you get yourself in such trouble, stranger?

Cecil Saltfish: It's me, Cecil Saltfish, the trader and I'm tied up to this tree . . . er . . . Bully Bullfrog did this when I sold more beads than he did.

Paw Paw: Well, I not going to untie you, Mr Saltfish, 'cos I afraid of Bullfrog bite.

Reader: And he hurried away.

Cecil Saltfish
& Reader: 'Help, Help,' shouted Cecil again.

Cecil Saltfish: It's me, Cecil Saltfish, the trader, and I'm tied up to this tree. Bully Bullfrog did this when he was jealous when I sold more beads than he did. Please untie me.

Yam: Me never untie you, Cecil Saltfish. As much as me like you, me afraid of Bullfrog bite.

Reader: And she hurried away leaving little Yam to keep up with her as best he could. Before Cecil could recover from his disappointment Plantain come past, bent and straining under the weight of a heavy basket.

Plantain: Why you tie up like that, Mister?

Cecil Saltfish: Because of Bullfrog. He tied me up to this tree when he . . . I . . . I sold more beads than he did. You see we both trade in beads. Please untie me.

Plantain: Well, I'm sorry, but me can't help you. You see, I afraid of of Bullfrog bite.

Although the original text contained some features of Jamaican Creole, it is interesting to note that the children's performance moves much closer to Creole than the text. This is all the more remarkable when you consider that only one of the five performers had links with the Caribbean while the other four included children of Greek and Turkish Cypriot origin and an indigenous Londoner. The important point about this exercise is that it allowed children who also happen to be fluent speakers of British English to demonstrate something of their range of language skills. These included not only an approximation to Jamaican Creole grammar and pronunciation, but also a well-developed sense of when different language varieties are appropriate.

Rhymes, riddles and rigmaroles

The Lore and Language of School Children by Iona and Peter Opie has been highly acclaimed in all quarters since its publication in 1959. Its reprint as a paperback (Paladin, 1977) points to the timeless quality and appeal of the world of children's rhymes, taunts and humour. The agent of transmission for the lore of children is, of course, the peer group. Friends and siblings rather than adults are the fountainhead of knowledge and sometimes perform a very supportive and directly didactic role in the learning process. Equally noteworthy is the speed of transmission. The Opies document how parodies of 'The Ballad of Davy Crockett', beginning 'The Yellow Rose of Texas', were collected in Perth in April 1956, in Alton, Battersea, Great Bookham, Reading and Scarborough in July 1956, in Kent in August 1956 and Swansea in September 1956. Remarkably, an Australian correspondent had reported a similar ditty sweeping Sydney schools the previous January. This transcontinental movement is all the more remarkable when you consider that the original 'Davy Crockett' song had only been launched on the radio at the beginning of 1956.

It is easy to understand the attraction of children's lore. It charts the development of verbal wit and the enjoyment of language for its own sake. It offers opportunities for poking fun at adults and gives children licence to explore taboo subjects. A version of the 'lady of Darjeeling, who weeweed all over the ceiling' which I recorded recently took some ten seconds to tell while the hysterical laughter which followed in its wake lasted a full minute. While the realm of the 'naughty' joke or story is arguably outside the classroom, there are many other aspects of the lore and language of school children which teachers can very usefully encourage.

Skipping, nursery and playground rhymes, for instance, are rich, diverse and universal. As an important part of the child's culture they can be tape-recorded, written down, illustrated and compared. Comparisons can be made between different countries and also different parts of the country. Equally interesting, children can find out if their rhymes and games are the same as their parents' or grandparents' and consider how they are transmitted from one generation to the next. A number of teachers have remarked to me recently that this aspect of children's culture has died or is dying, particularly in multicultural inner city schools. Several student teachers with whom I was working set out to find if this was true. They returned with pages of transcripts of children's playground rhymes, skipping rhymes and jokes. Certain activities like skipping are, of course, seasonal and junior age children have a much more impressive repertoire than those in the first school. These provisos apart, the lore and language of school children would appear to be very much alive in the inner city streets and playgrounds.

Children's jokes are another underestimated classroom resource. A joke has to have a proper sequence of events and a good punchline to succeed. It also requires the development of a wide range of stylistic effects if it is to make the maximum impact on an audience. Yet the sequencing and stylistic development which characterize an activity universally acclaimed by children are the very qualities which teachers try to encourage in children's writing. Take 6 year old Sally's albeit rather unsuccessful attempt to tell the story of the 100% polar bear:

> Sally: There was three polar bears: a mummy bear, a baby bear and a daddy bear. One day the baby bear asked his mummy, 'Am I a 100% bear?' and his mummy said, 'Yes'. 'Am I . . . um . . . what is it Jack?
> Jack: 'Am I a 100% polar bear?'
> Sally: 'Am I a 100% polar bear?' 'Ask your father,' said mummy bear. So he went and asked his father: 'Am I a 100% bear?' 'Yes', said the father. 'Well why am I so flipping cold?'

Although not executed with very great finesse, there are many encouraging signs of incipient narrative skills in Sally's joke. The sequencing is good, although one suspects the punchline might have been delivered somewhat differently. There are specific story-telling markers like 'There was . . .', 'one day' and, most interestingly, the subject-verb inversion in 'said mummy bear', 'said his father', etc. And her use of connectives goes beyond the omnipresent 'and' which characterizes most young children's writing.

Sally's 9 year old brother Jack shows considerably more sophistication:

> Newsflash! Newsflash!
> Three people have escaped from the Tiddletown prison and police . . . they got out in helicopters . . . using armed weapons . . . and police have set up roadblocks and can't understand why they evaded them . . . how they evaded them.
>
> Newsflash! Newsflash!
> Four beds have been stolen from a warehouse in Tiddletown now and police . . . police say they will spring into action.

Jack tells the joke haltingly and sometimes makes mistakes (e.g. 'using armed weapons'). Yet he makes an impressive attempt at reproducing the vocabulary of crime reports ('roadblocks', 'evaded', 'spring into action'). He also makes use of the passive construction ('have been stolen') which is relatively rare in children of his age.

Stories and storytelling

Today, most people in Britain associate stories with books and the written word. This was brought home to me very clearly in an incident at my son's school in which the hometime story had been told, rather than read, by one of the parents. All but one of the children got up to leave at the end. When asked why she was not getting ready to go home, she replied that she was waiting for the story! We tend to speak of reading and telling stories almost interchangeably and yet the two activities are very different. When we read a story we are very much restricted to the text and there is little latitude for individual interpretation. When we tell a story it becomes something of a dramatic performance. There are variations in rhythms, stress and tone of voice, and pauses, gestures and facial expressions which can never adequately be captured by the punctuation marks and italics of the written medium. And, whereas reading a story is a relatively pedestrian experience which can vary only within strict limits imposed upon the reader, the teller can respond to both the audience and the situation in such a way that each performance is different from the last.

The tremendous importance attached to the written word in our society means that story telling tends to be a highly under-rated activity. Yet there are very many societies where story telling is part of the fabric of everyday life for adults and children alike and verbal skills of all descriptions are highly prized. Such skills enable people to establish themselves in the pecking order as adolescents or define their status in the community as adults. In many parts of the world today, from Africa to China and Cyprus to Mexico, it is possible to find a village storyteller practising his art in a bar or café or some other meeting place. Such a person is a highly respected member of society. Contrary to common assumption, only the bare bones of the story are transmitted from generation to generation in pre-literate communities of this kind. It is left to the teller to build upon this framework and certain individuals are clearly more skilled than others.

Some teachers in multicultural primary schools have been quick to recognize the importance of such skills and have invited parents to tell stories on a regular basis. Asian and other bilingual parents will tend to work with small groups of children from their own communities. West Indian parents have been used to tell stories either to the whole class or to mixed groups of children. Initiatives of this kind can be valuable on a number of different fronts. Ethnic minority adults are seen by all children to be in a position of authority and respect in the classroom. Minority children thus have access to a wider range of roles of adult figures on which to model themselves; indigenous children realize that ethnic minority adults can fulfil the same range of roles as English speaking white people. Equally important, children hear their own language in the school context and there is a useful challenge to the traditional dichotomy in which standard English is the prestigious language of the classroom and other languages and dialects are considered as of low status and are relegated to the playground and the street.

Nor is storytelling an experience which should be reserved exclusively for young children. Mike Rosen (1982), for instance, recounts some interesting experiences of his while writer-in-residence at Vauxhall Manor school, which have as much relevance for secondary as for primary teachers:

> Elaine's sister Judith had told something like eight or nine Anansi stories on tape - some of which we made into booklets - before it occurred to me that we could lend her a tape-recorder and ask her to record her mother. This she did. Her mother, an 'ordinary' working class woman, is as fine a storyteller as anyone anywhere. You don't have to go to the Brothers Grimm, or to this or that Book of Beautiful Tales. Great storytellers are amongst us. If you have some of these stories on tape and play them in school, what happens? The parents' culture becomes part of the school curriculum - even if it's only for five minutes at a time. And there was Farrah too, who speaks Punjabi at home and told me she didn't like stories, who told me she only really liked books on magnetism, but who finally let on that her grandmother tells her stories. The result of that is a tape of an old lady telling an epic in Punjabi which Farrah translated for us. (p. 389)

Equally important, storytelling is a skill which can be encouraged in children and it can be a particularly valuable exercise with slow readers and children with learning difficulties. Take Jennifer, the 13 year old daughter of Barbadian parents who was born in Britain. At the time she wrote the essay reproduced opposite she had been receiving remedial help for a number of years, and her writing was still technically very weak. Her oral rendering of the same story, however, creates a very different impression. The transcript below overcomes the poor presentation of the original essay, though obviously it cannot communicate the fast fluent delivery, the modulations in her tone of voice, the pauses, stresses and facial expressions of the actual telling. It nonetheless leaves the reader in no doubt at all that the story is an extremely dramatic and humorous one:

The new people next door

Part 1

I was Saturday morning. nosy old hilda knok on our back door. "Morning mrs small" how are you today? "alright" said my mum "by the way / see you have new neighbour" "how do you now" said my mum "I was happen to be looking through the curtains" "you are always looking through the curtains" say my mum. They look a snoby looking lot" said hilda "are they sit their" said my mum. "their" yes she said Hilda. we went out to see them. "they do look rather snoby" said my mum. "I told you so" said hilda. "mind my funter" said the lady. "mind my cold fish" said the man. try to do n't broke my my best vas said they lady. "mummy, Mummy" said the little girl. he pulled my pony tail

Part 2.

"naughty little". said the woman "I told I told you more than I time we should come to America for our hoilday O no he said O no it go let go to reading reading and here we are surrowndy by scruffy people" no! "how dear she" "how dear she" "how dear you call us scruff" no but, no buts from you. you horriable selfish ongrapfull unkind woman". said hilda. "how dear you call me a unkind, horriable woman you showed not had said that" dont steand they Alfred and let this woman call me name. "yes" don't called her name" "is that all you can say" well I am leaveing come a long sally" we mymum hilda and laughter the hole day.

The New Neighbours

It was Saturday morning and Hilda come and knock on our back door.

'Morning, Mrs Small,' she said.

'Morning, Hilda,' said my mum.

'Anyway, I see you've got some snobby neighbours next door.'

'How do you know?' said my mum.

'Oh, I just been looking through my curtains', said Hilda.

'You always looking through your curtains', said my mum.

'Anyway, they're still out there?' said my mum.

'Oh, yes,' said Hilda.

We went outside to meet our snobby neighbours.

'Oh mind my furniture', said the woman.

'Mind my goldfish', said the man.

'Mummy, mummy, mummy that boy pulled my pontails!'

'Naughty little boy! . . . I told you let's go to America. But no, you insist let's go to Reading. "Nice people round here", you said, "nice fashion people. Oh, they so lovely!" But now we surrounded by this scruffy lot and unkind.'

'How dare you call us scruffy lot! We nice people round here. We are nice and good people round here. What are you talking about? You the unkind and scruffy lot. You come round here making trouble about our street.'

'Alfred, do something!'

'Yes, don't insult my wife!'

'Is that all you have to say? Is that all you have to say?'

'Now I'm going. I'm not going to stand here to be insulted by this woman. Come on Sally, let's go.'

Me and my mum and Hilda we went inside and we laughed about that the whole day.

In one activity, Jennifer is a failure; in the other she is startling success. The poor technique of the written version may even lead a harassed teacher marking the second pile of exercise books at the end of the school day to overlook the lively characterization and great inherent wit in the story. The teacher who encourages the child's abilities is in a much better position to deal with the technical weaknesses of the written version. Children are far more likely to be receptive to advice about the presentation of a piece of work when confident that the teacher respects and values what they have to say and their ability as story tellers. Michael Rosen (1982) describes the problem of children like Jennifer in very graphic terms:

To be a story-teller in the secondary school sounds a bit like a rebuke - a liar, a boaster, a rabble rouser, back of the coach entertainer. To produce a totally legible hand-written account or story has normally had to involve quite a few hours logged up of spelling, punctuation, letter-formation and comprehension exercises to reach a time when the gap between what you *want* to say and what you have the *mechanical ability* to say becomes bearably narrow, i.e. when to say something in writing isn't one hell of a grind. (p. 383)

He also points to ways in which the traditional hierarchy of Talk, Writing, Printing and Writing can be usefully challenged to the benefit of children with a story to tell. Tape recorders with rewind buttons, typewriters, paper, staple guns, even offset litho printing machines in some cases, are part of the standard school equipment which can make it possible for a told story to become a booklet circulating freely among any group within a school within a matter of days. There is a tremendous potential for schools to build up their own library of oral culture – whether on tape or in booklet form – both as a stimulus for further work of all kinds and purely and simply as good entertainment.

Summary

Until relatively recent times, the role of children's talk in learning has received very little attention in educational circles. Regardless of the age of the children in question, teachers tend to monopolize classroom talk and to control both the quantity and kind of language produced by pupils. Yet 'talk' and 'chat' are quite distinct and the encouragement of classroom talk is in no way a formula for chaos. On the contrary, talk can facilitate the development of linguistic and conceptual skills, as well as fostering certain social skills and moral attitudes. This realization offers the teacher many opportunities for drawing on the wide range of 'speech events' which are a normal part of children's culture, but which are usually undervalued or ignored. Very often, it is also possible to tap the special skills of non-English and dialect speaking children. The advantages of working in this way are two-fold: first, the children themselves are likely to gain from the feeling that their language and culture have a valued place in school life; second, teachers are likely to have a heightened awareness of the child's existing skills and ability to learn.

7 Children reading

The reading process

Learning to read is a complex process which is as difficult to describe as the process of learning to speak, and there have been many misconceptions about the acquisition of both speech and reading. Learning to speak, for instance, was often thought to be simply a matter of imitation and repetition of adult models. However, over the years, we have come to understand that children construct their own systems of rules, or grammars, which gradually approximate more and more closely to the adult norm. Forms like *I goed* and *it's mine's* are certainly not heard from parents or other adults, but they do provide evidence of a capacity to recognize and generalize patterns in the speech around them and this is a prerequisite for language learning. By the same token, reading cannot be considered a process of decoding each word. Fluent readers are engaged in what one researcher (Goodman in Gollasch, 1982) has termed 'a psycholinguistic guessing game'.

When you consider that it can take up to four times as long to read a passage aloud as it does to read it silently it becomes obvious that something far more complex than word by word decoding is taking place. It would seem that the eye picks out certain key pieces of information and that the brain fills in the rest. Although we can only speculate as to the precise nature of the reading process and how children learn to read, the analysis of oral reading can give some very useful pointers. Take, for instance, the following extract from an 11 year old's attempts to come to terms with a rather difficult reading passage (Neale, 1958). Where the text is crossed out, the word(s) written above represent the child's attempt to make meaning of the passage:

<pre>
                    driver
1   Meanwhile a ~~diver~~ with technical equipment for their release
    was in peril. His life-line had become entangled around
              projection on
3   a ~~projection on~~ an adjacent wreckage. Experience warned him
</pre>

2. dislodge
1. disknowledge
against his first impulse to ~~dislodge~~ the line by force.
5 Patiently he turned and twisted. At last his calmness and
                                                  that
  persistence were rewarded. Triumphantly he detached ~~the~~
                          X   he
7 final loop from the obstruction. Then fatigued ~~but~~ undaunted
    his
  by ~~this~~ unpleasant accident he proceeded to provide an escape
9 for the submarine's captives.
    [X=refusal]

This reader shows evidence of just how various cue systems operate in the reading process. Note the substitution of *that* for *the* in line 6 and *his* for *this* in line 8. It is significant that in both cases the substitute can fill the same grammatical slot in the sentence as the original word, without changing the meaning of the passage. The word *driver* has obviously been confused with *diver* in line 1 because of their graphic similarity, but it is nonetheless significant that they are both nouns. The substitution of *project of* for *projection on* in line 3 suggests a similar process. Line 4 illustrates an interesting example of strategies used in successfully reading an unfamiliar word. Her first attempt - *disknowledge* - bears some graphic resemblance to *dislodge* but she realizes that this word is either unlikely or impossible and this modifies her guess. The substitution of *he* for *but* in line 7 is equally revealing. Note that she could not read *fatigued* and probably does not know what it means. It is also very likely that she is unsure of the meaning of *undaunted*. She wrongly identifies the -ed suffix as a verb ending and in order to make sense of the sentence provides it with a subject, *he*. Clearly, this child is making use of grammatical and semantic as well as graphic information in reading the passage.

In the light of this kind of analysis it is more accurate to talk, as Goodman does, in terms of reading *miscues* rather than mistakes. It also becomes clear that, while miscue is a useful general label, readers reveal a wide range of miscues. Various analyses have been proposed by different writers. They vary in degree of detail and ease with which they can be applied. For instance, one particularly useful framework for the classification and codification of miscues has been proposed by Southgate, Arnold & Johnson (1981) (see Table 4). The theoretical model on which this classification is based draws not only on textual information but also on the readers' knowledge of grammar and feeling about whether something is probable or improbable. Substitutions are particularly interesting in this respect, since they

Table 4: *Classification of miscues*

Original text	Miscue	Coding symbol	Explanation
Mrs Bird's contribution	Non-response	<u>contribution</u>	Prompting required
made a point of keeping	Hesitation	made a point of/keeping	Hesitation, but word finally supplied
whether to have them	Repetition	whether to <u>have them</u>	Underlined word or phrase repeated (1 repetition)
It was Mr Brown	Self-correction	It was M̶r̶s̶ Mr Brown	Substitutes or makes other error, but then supplies right word
a more complicated signal	Substitution	a more c̶o̶m̶p̶l̶i̶c̶a̶t̶e̶d̶ complashant signal	Substitutes one word for another
fell out of bed	Insertion	fell out of/ the bed	Inserts word or phrase
peering out at the garden	Omission	peering out (at) the garden	Omits word or phrase
to have one drawn	Reversal	<u>one/drawn</u>	Reverses word or phrase

Source: Southgate et al. (1981) p. 269

may or may not be graphically similar to the original word, or syntactically and semantically identical with it. They therefore show more clearly than any other kind of miscue the different levels of language on which the reader draws.

Such a model has far-reaching practical implications. For instance, a problem solving approach to reading which requires children to use all the information at their disposal to arrive at an unknown word is likely to be more appropriate than one which aims to develop purely mechanical decoding skills. Teachers who intervene in the middle of children's reading may well be hindering the development of such problem solving strategies. They may also detract from the child's pleasure in books by suggesting that the main object of the exercise is to foster perfectionist skills. A far more reflective approach to teacher intervention is thus in order if we are to encourage a problem solving approach to reading. A useful framework is provided, for example, by Moon & Raban (1980).

Question	*Intervention*
1 Is the text too difficult generally? i.e. miscue rate is higher than 1 word in 20.	Suggest less difficult text
2. Is the word a special noun like the name of someone or somewhere?	Tell child the word.
3. Is the word outside the child's experience?	Ask child what he thinks word *should* be – what fits the meaning. If he offers word with same meaning accept it and tell him word refused is ____ and that it means same as word he has supplied.
4. Is the word difficult to decode but within child's experience?	(a) Tell him to read to end of sentence/end of line/to next full stop, whichever suits text and child's understanding. Then go back to beginning of sentence and try to fit word in context. *Or* Tell him to start sentence again – get it 'on the run'. Draw attention to illustration. Read up to problem word yourself using exaggerated intonation.
	(b) Ask child what he thinks word *should* be – what could fit the sense. Then as for 3 above.
	(c) Draw attention to initial consonant and link with (b)
	(d) Draw attention to syllables and known words within the word (e.g. *cat*amaran) and link with (b) and (c).
	(e) If all else fails, tell him the word!

Dialect and reading

The kind of problem solving approach suggested in the work of Gollasch (1982), Smith (1976), Moon & Raban (1980) and many other specialists in the field of reading applies to all children. Dialect speakers, however, are faced with additional difficulties which deserve special attention. There is a considerable body of research which shows that reading failure is most prevalent among children from working class and ethnic minority families. Although there is not necessarily a causative relationship, these children are speakers of a language or dialect other than standard English. Because of the central importance assumed by reading in education, reading achievement has sometimes been used as a measure of general educational performance and non-standard speakers, particularly those from ethnic minority backgrounds, have been shown repeatedly to lag behind in their reading. The 1969 interim report of the ILEA Literacy Survey, for instance, showed that at the beginning of the second year of primary school four times as many indigenous children (12 per cent) as immigrants (3 per cent) were good readers and almost twice as many immigrant children (28.5 per cent) were 'poor readers' compared with native English children. Subsequent reports on the performance of ethnic minority children have tended to concentrate on streaming and examination results. However, in view of the relationship between reading and academic achievement, it seems highly likely that the continuing patterns of under-performance among ethnic minority children are also reflected in their levels of reading achievement.

Attitudes towards dialect and reading have changed considerably over the years. Until the sixties, no attention was given to their special relationship at all. Then, in the search for causes of school failure and, in particular, reading failure, linguists provided a simple and – as it transpired – overly simplistic solution: inner city children, particularly black children, spoke a dialect of English which differed significantly from the standard English of reading materials. The further removed this dialect was from the standard, the greater the difficulties the child would encounter in learning to read. In an American context, one solution to this problem was to produce reading programmes in Black English. However, this approach met with considerable criticism, not least from black parents who felt this represented yet another attempt to hold their children back.

It is not at all clear if dialect reading programmes can or did raise reading levels. Dillard (1978: 308), for instance, holds that the research in this area is inconclusive and that 'most of the projects have been so badly planned that even positive results from one of them would be virtually meaningless'. Much of the enthusiasm for Black English reading materials seems to derive from an inadequate understanding of the reading process. All dialect speakers tend to translate a standard text into their own dialect. A West Indian child, for instance, might read:

All the *boy run* home

for

All the *boys ran* home.

British working class children from many parts of the country might read:

I *seen* him do it

for

I *saw* him do it

or

I *come* in straightaway

for

I *came* in straightaway.

Such dialect-based miscues demonstrate very healthy reading strategies. They show that children are making use of their knowledge of the language to predict what comes next and have obviously understood the meaning of the text. All too often, however, the teacher intervenes and insists on a standard English form. Berdan (1981): 220) describes the devastating impact which interruptions of this kind can have on children:

> Their effect on the continuity of reading instruction is deadening. Children learn to cope by reading slower so that they will encounter fewer possible interruptions, by reading at a barely audible level so that teachers cannot determine exactly what was said or simply by refusing to read at all.

It would seem that teacher attitudes towards language differences are far more critical than the differences themselves. For in drawing attention to dialect-based miscues, the teacher risks giving the impression that the main object of the exercise is to read for accuracy rather than meaning, and is helping to form a child who barks at print. Goodman & Buck (1973: 11-12) summarize the situation thus:

> In encouraging divergent speakers to use their linguistic competence, both receptive and productive, and accepting their dialect-based miscues, we minimize the effect of dialect differences. In rejecting their dialects we maximize the effect.

Research into reading and dialect throughout the sixties and early seventies tended to focus on linguistic and psychological variables to the exclusion of larger educational issues which affect achievement. Venezky (1981), for instance, draws attention to the fact that the education of inner city children is affected not only by language differences but by fewer resources, higher teacher and pupil absenteeism and less home and community support, He also points out that case studies of inner city schools that succeed in teaching reading emphasize organisational variables, such as careful monitoring of student progress and positive attitudes towards students, rather than 'treatment' of dialect differences. Harber (1981) in a review of research findings on reading failure, suggests that there is no *one* cause, but rather multiple factors in combination.

Yet, although the suggestion that dialect differences in themselves are great enough to cause reading difficulties now seems naive and oversimplistic, the emphasis on non-standard dialect continues to serve a number of very important educational functions. There is a growing understanding of the symbolic role of the language which children bring to school and the wisdom of teaching standard English as an alternative to the dialect rather than as a substitute for it. By the same token, there is increasing awareness of the part which linguistic features play in stereotyping and the dangers of translating stereotypes into reality.

Such an awareness has even achieved legal recognition in an American court case. Lawyers for some eleven children classed as retarded contended that, in attempting to teach standard English, the school had failed to give credence to the language of the home. This, they claimed, had resulted in frustration and withdrawal by the pupils and had ultimately led to their classification as retarded. A US district judge ruled that the school had not properly fulfilled its legal and professional obligations to the children and ordered special in-service programmes on language variation for the 28 teachers in the children's school. This judgement, of course, begs a number of important questions. Who is responsible for the teacher's ignorance – the school authority, teacher trainers or the teachers themselves? What about all the teachers in other schools who are equally ignorant? Can you legislate a change in attitude? None the less, the 'Ann Arbor case' established an important legal principle, namely that methods of dealing with the children's home language which frustrate them and cause them to withdraw are in violation of the law.

Reading as a culturally alien activity

We have developed a school system in which white, male-dominated middle class language and values have until recently remained unchallenged. A great deal has been written about the sexist, racist and classist bias of books, materials and the hidden curriculum of schools (Dixon, 1977; Jeffcoate, 1979; Hoffman, 1981). It is now widely, though not universally, recognized that many children find it difficult to identify with the suburban-semi-detached-with-garden-and-garage world inhabited by generations of reading scheme heroes and their two parent nuclear families. Great improvements have taken place in the last ten years. Reading schemes like *Breakthrough, Nippers* and *Sparks* (though not exempt from criticism) have broken the stranglehold of Janet and John and Peter and Jane, though according to Grundin (1980) the newer schemes are not in use in many schools. Storybooks and novels, too, have begun to reflect the multiracial and multicultural composition of present day Britain, although they sometimes fall into the trap of tokenism - a solitary figure in the background who plays no part in the story - and sometimes they portray girls or working class or ethnic minority people in a stereotyped way. And, while the number and quality of suitably 'multicultural' books has increased considerably, they still form only a tiny proportion of all the books available.

There are certainly indications that the use of culturally relevant materials has a positive effect on children's reading achievement. C. Grant (1973), for instance, established that Black American children who used the SRA *We are Black* self-instructional materials performed significantly better on a standardized reading test than control group children who used conventional materials. In another study, G. Grant (1974) also found statistically significant differences in reading achievement and reading attitudes in favour of children who had used culturally relevant materials. The content of reading materials, however, constitutes only one aspect of a complex problem.

A number of writers, including Labov & Robins (1972), Carter (1971) and Berdan (1981) have drawn attention to the mismatch between current teaching practice and black children's concept of teacher-pupil behaviour and learning style. The Labov and Robins' study, although small scale, is of particular interest inasmuch as it shows very clearly the relationship between language, culture and reading. Out of a sample of 32 boys identified as non-members of the street culture, several were on grade and some were even ahead of grade. Yet out of a sample of 46 boys who were members of street gangs, no-one was reading ahead of grade and only one was reading on grade. Labov & Robins suggest that culture conflict is a strong factor in reading failure. It seems inevitable that one of the consequences of being told that nearly everything you say is wrong is to reject the values of the school - and this includes learning to read - rather than to adopt forms which seem alien.

The school environment and school values are plainly not influencing the boys firmly grounded in street culture . . . Teachers in city schools have little ability to reward or punish members of the street culture or to motivate learning by any means (p.252).

Sometimes the desire to be seen identifying with the values of peer group culture rather than those of the school becomes exaggerated into an elaborate charade. Cheshire (1982a) reports the case of a boy whom she heard reading extracts from a James Bond novel to friends at a Reading adventure playground, but who was in a remedial reading group at school. Herbert Kohl in *Thirty Six Children* recounts similar cases in New York.

Reading and bilinguals
Given the discussion of the reading process in preceding sections, it would seem largely a matter of commonsense that it should be easier to learn to read in the mother tongue than in a second language. The translation of theory into practice in city schools where children come from a wide range of language backgrounds would, however, pose insuperable problems. It is also interesting to note the controversial nature of research findings on the subject of which language should be used in teaching bilingual children to read. Commonsense solutions can sometimes be both impractical and simplistic.

Barrera-Vásquez (1953), Österberg (1961), Downing (1978) and many other writers, drawing on research in a number of countries, consider that serious retardation occurs in the development of literacy when children are taught through the medium of a second language. This position would seem to gain support from Troike's (1978) review of findings from a wide range of bilingual programmes, which concludes that the level of English skills achieved by children educated in the mother tongue is as high or higher than those educated exclusively through the medium of English. On the other hand, Lambert & Tucker (1972) and Giles (1971) report that children in French-Canadian 'immersion programs' achieve the same level of reading in their mother tongue as children who attend 'normal schools' by the time they finish elementary school. Ramos et al. (1967) and Cohen et al. (1973) also suggest that the language of initial literacy does not significantly affect achievement in English literacy. Engles (1975), reviewing some 25 studies of the effects of using the mother tongue or a second language as the medium of instruction found no consistent trends.

Non-linguistic factors also play a part in the acquisition of literacy in bilinguals. It is very noticeable that, in all parts of the world, the bilingual children who underperform in school are those immigrant or ethnic minority children who are in the process of being assimilated by a dominant majority and not those who belong to majority language groups. In a British context, for instance, Punjabi speaking children who learn English tend to underperform whereas English speaking children who receive a Welsh medium education have a record of high academic achievement. In a North American context, children from English speaking families who receive a French medium education do better than Navajo and Puerto Rican children educated in English.

There is a widespread assumption that we have only a limited linguistic capacity so that bilinguals will inevitably perform less well than monolinguals. Such an explanation is consistent with the underachievement of ethnic minority bilinguals. It cannot, however, account for the high level of performance of other bilingual children. As we saw in Chapter Two, Cummins (1981) has proposed a Common Underlying Proficiency model to account for the discrepancy between the two sets of findings. Correlational studies of certain cognitive and academic skills in children's first and second languages strongly suggest that there is a basic proficiency which underlies the processing of meanings in both languages and that experience with either language can promote the development of proficiency underlying both languages. Such a model can, of course, account for both the satisfactory performance in English of Navajo children taught basic literacy skills through the medium of the mother tongue and the equally high level of achievement of English speaking children taught to read through the medium of Welsh. In order to understand children who underperform in the second language, however, we need to look at factors such as motivation and exposure to the language.

Reading behaviour of children for whom English is a second language

Children from different linguistic backgrounds show a continuum of reading behaviour. Those who are monolingual speakers of another language will only be able to respond to English writing to the extent that they may happen to be literate in another language which uses the same script. Those children who speak English fluently, on the other hand, will behave in exactly the same way as native speakers. Between these two poles, children's reading will faithfully reflect both the relative influence of the mother tongue and the gradual progression towards control over English phonology, orthography, grammar, vocabulary and idiom.

Studies which focus specifically on the reading behaviour of children in a second language are rare. The fullest accessible treatment of this area is to be found in Goodman, Goodman & Flores (1979). Although designed primarily for American teachers familiar with bilingual education programmes, a good deal of its discussion is relevant to British teachers working with children for whom English is a second language. They suggest that second language learners exhibit three main patterns of reading behaviour:

1. Noticeable but superficial differences, in which case the process can still be relatively efficient and effective.
2. Limitations in the ability of readers to express what they have understood in English.
3. Some disruption to comprehension which may be minor or severe.

The first pattern of reading behaviour is most commonly marked by the omission of inflectional endings. Take, for instance, the passage below read by Zaffar after eighteen months in England. Deviations from the text are indicated above the words in question:

```
1 Honk is a car horn.
2 The car is very old.
3 Honk is very new.
   Mrs         drive
4 Miss Stubbs drives the car.
             push
5 When she pushes a button
6 Honk hoots.
7 Too-oo-oot Too-oo-oot.
   Mrs        don't
8 Miss Stubbs does not go fast.
      don't
9 She does not go fast round corners.
      don't           buzzy street
10 She does not go fast in busy streets.
11 She stops when someone steps into the street.
```

It is interesting to note, however, that Zaffar's tendency to omit inflectional endings (e.g. *drive* for *drives* in line 4) does not affect the meaning of the passage, and even inappropriate pronunciations such as *buzzy* for *busy* often have only a minimal effect on the child's attempt to draw meaning from what he or she is reading. Goodman, Goodman & Flores, for instance, report the case of Arab children reading a story about ploughing. Few of the children pronounced the word correctly when it appeared in the story, yet all of them were able to describe a plough and the activity of ploughing when they retold the story either in Arabic or in English.

The second pattern of reading behaviour – limitations in the ability of readers to express what they have understood in English – also tends to give rise to more teacher concern than is necessary. All too often we confuse receptive and productive control of language, assuming that what a child says is a faithful reflection of what he or she understands. Receptive competence in a language, however, far outstrips production and second language learners understand far more speech and writing than they can actually produce. This becomes especially clear when children are questioned or given the opportunity to retell a story in the mother tongue, as in the case of the Arabic children and the discussion of ploughing.

The final pattern – some disruption to comprehension which may be minor or severe – is, of course, of more concern to both teachers and children. Goodman, Goodman & Flores suggest that this is a problem which may derive in part from teaching methods:

> There is too much concern for form without function, too much tradition and too little relevance, too much focus on skill and not enough on comprehension, too much making kids adapt to the curriculum rather than adapting the curriculum to the kids. That is not good for any learners; for bilinguals it can be tragic. (p.36).

It is encouraging to note that many of the strategies which can usefully be employed to help bilingual children overcome limitations in understanding are also helpful to bidialectal and monolingual speakers.

Positive teacher strategies in the teaching of reading

Our understanding of the reading process has grown considerably in recent years. We still have a good way to go, however, in the translation of newly acquired knowledge into sound classroom practice. The special position of children who speak a non-standard dialect of English, or English as a second language, is a question which researchers and practitioners have considered in even less depth. None the less, a number of observations can usefully be made at this point. It would appear, for instance, that all children, irrespective of their linguistic background, apply similar strategies to reading tasks. In the case of successful readers, all the information at their disposal – graphical, grammatical and semantic – is used in an attempt to predict what comes next and to draw meaning from a text. However, speakers of English as a second language (and, to a much lesser extent, those children for whom standard English is a second dialect) are at a disadvantage in making sense of what they read, because they do not have access to the same cue systems as standard English speakers whose language is closest to that of written English.

A number of practical approaches to the teaching of reading are likely to be helpful to all children. For speakers of English as a second language, however, these approaches are particularly important.

1. *Reading to children* is a very helpful practice. It prepares them for encounters with a variety of styles in their own reading. It also allows for questioning in order to establish whether they have understood key words or concepts. Discussion of the story before or after the reading helps children to draw meaning from what they hear. Because it can be very enjoyable to listen to a story, it helps to promote the idea of reading as an interesting and useful activity. Reading to children is especially important in the early years of school, but there is no reason why it should be restricted to this stage.

2. *Do not interrupt unnecessarily in the reading process* (see pp. 98-9). Repeated teacher intervention detracts from the problem solving approach to reading which we want to encourage. It falsely creates the impression that the main purpose is reading for accuracy rather than reading for meaning.

3. *Teaching explicitly about the reading process can be extremely valuable.* Children should be helped to understand that it is legitimate to predict when reading and that reading must make sense. It should be made clear that the significant part of reading is the search for meaning rather than simply decoding each word as it appears on the page. Two kinds of exercise are particularly well suited to helping children achieve this end. The first is called Cloze Procedure and involves deleting words at regular intervals – usually every fifth or seventh word – from a passage.

> Little did Mr Dizzy know that_____drinks deeply from the water at_____wishing well, his wish will come_____.
> And Mr Dizzy had wished that_____could be clever.
> And his wish_____came true.
> He was clever.
> But_____didn't know it.
> Not yet!

Children are encouraged to make use of the information in the text – both what comes before the deleted word and what comes after – in an attempt to guess what it might be. The high success rate shows them that reading unknown words is a question of thoughtful and informed rather than wild and random guesswork.

In the second kind of exercise a frequently recurring unknown or nonsense word, significant to the meaning, is inserted in the text. Dialect passages can be very useful in this respect, since they help promote the idea that something is not necessarily difficult or impossible to understand simply because it is different. Take, for instance, this extract from a story about Natty Dread by Steve Hoyle:

> Thus Natty addressed the ministers who were somewhat startled by his wild appearance and flowing locks but who never the less listened to all he had to say.
>
> 'I man a rid dis town fe rat! Me a do it wid sounds! But I and I band just a lickle bit short of dunny. If unu promise fe pay me den come mek we start now!'
>
> The Prime Minister and his cabinet were delighted with Natty's words. They eagerly promised him the sum of one million pounds if he could rid the city of rats. Natty considered this for a minute . . . . 'Tank yu', sah, 'he said addressing the Prime Minister, 'dat dunny sound fine for I but what yu' woulda pay fe I and I band?'

What is *dunny?* What is *unu?* Why does Natty say *I and I?* In exercises of this kind children can discuss the concepts they have built up and the cues in the text which they used to arrive at meaning. This encourages them to carry on reading when they come across an unknown word and to understand that meaning is derived from the total context and not a word in isolation.

4. *It is important to work with material which interests a child.* Very often one or two unknown words can reduce a passage to a meaningless jumble, particularly in the case of second language learners. The temptation is for the teacher to choose material well within the reading range of a child. It is certainly important in normal circumstances that children should not be exposed to books which fall within their frustration level (usually defined as one unknown word in ten). However, this is not the only criterion that should guide the choice of material. Interest in a special character or theme should always be taken into account and, when motivation is strong, quite astonishing results can be achieved. Hoyle (1978), for instance, describes the development of the Natty Dread materials from which the extract above was taken. In the first instance he read the stories to his children who went on to produce illustrations of the various scenes. He then produced the stories in booklet form, complete with the children's illustrations. All the children enjoyed the stories very much, presumably because they identified strongly with Natty and felt that the stories belonged to them. One interesting development, however, concerns a number of poor readers who surprised everybody by persevering with the stories and reading them from start to finish. Several of these children, now in secondary school, have returned to see Steve Hoyle and have said quite openly that it

was the Natty stories which really got them started as readers.

Nor should the role of reading in the acquisition of a second language be underestimated. It offers the same range of opportunities as speech for the learner to make hypotheses about the rules of language and to deduce the meanings of words and idioms. Unlike speech, however, there is considerable scope for reviewing the language input. Whereas it is embarassing to ask for a speaker to repeat a message when it is not understood, rereading presents no difficulty. And children who for cultural or other reasons shy away from interpersonal contact, may find reading a far more comfortable source of language than speech.

5. *Reading should be promoted as a functional and integral part of the curriculum* rather than as an isolated activity. It is very important that children should be given the opportunity to see reading as a useful, interesting and enjoyable activity. One of the ways in which this can be achieved is to ensure that reading is an integral part of a wide range of activities and does not always start and finish as an activity in its own right. We are obviously talking in terms of an approach to reading rather than a particular reading scheme.

The 'Reading Through Understanding' project undertaken at the ILEA Centre for Urban Educational Studies has produced two sets of materials which neatly illustrate the general approach: *Make-a-Story* and *Share-a-Story*. *Make-a-Story* is aimed at 5-8 year olds and is a series of stories about children living in a multiracial urban setting. *Share-a-story* is a collection of folk tales from Africa and the Caribbean. Both sets of material have been designed to be used in several different ways – by the teacher for storytelling; by individual children either with cassette support or by themselves as their reading ability increases; and with groups of varying sizes with the teacher's help or independently.

A wide range of related activities is suggested for the materials. Children can retell the stories to a group or record them on a cassette for other children to listen to. Some children may want to write down their own version of the stories they have heard or recount related experiences of their own. These can be tape-recorded, written by the children themselves or dictated to the teacher. They can be made into books and wall stories for others to enjoy, as an activity for an individual, a group or even the whole class. The stories often lend themselves to role play and dramatization. Certain characters become so popular that children will want to write their own stories about them and enjoy illustrating incidents from the story. Older children like creating 'comic strip' versions of the stories and these can be given to younger children to read. Model making of animals, people and objects in the stories can provide useful experience at all levels.

Visits to places featured in the stories – a market, a building site, an adventure playground, a park – can make them even more interesting and lead on to other activities. The market story, for instance, might lead to children drawing up a shopping list of ingredients for particular recipes and visiting a local market to buy them. Food in fact plays an important part in many of the stories and parents or older brothers and sisters may be able to come into the school to show children how to prepare some typical Caribbean dishes.

Finally, the fact that the *Share-a-Story* materials are read on cassette by actors with different accents, and that Cantonese and Bengali phrases are included in some of the *Make-a-Story* materials, gives the opportunity for children who speak these (and other) languages and dialects to be recognized by the class as having a special skill. Interest in linguistic diversity can be used as a springboard for the enjoyment of poems, stories, songs and games in different languages and dialects.

Summary

Reading presents similar problems and challenges for all children, irrespective of their language backgrounds, and similar teacher strategies are required at all stages of development. To make sense of what they read, children draw on graphic, syntactic and semantic information, and insert or omit words in a way which demonstrates that they are internalizing the text and re-encoding it in their own language. This pattern is particularly marked in the case of bilingual and dialect speaking children whose language differs most strikingly from the standard English of most reading texts. The most appropriate teacher reponse is thus not to demand word for word accuracy but to recognize this kind of behaviour as a positive step in the direction of reading fluency.

The content and context of reading also deserve consideration. If children are to be motivated to learn, reading must be seen as an interesting, enjoyable and meaningful activity. This requires a move away from the monolingual and monocultural materials which dominate most schools and classrooms, and the development of activities and situations in which reading can be seen to be functional, rather than simply an end in itself.

8 Children writing

Writing and learning to write

We have already looked at the question of children talking. It might be tempting to look upon writing as the transcription of talk, but close examination shows it to be considerably more complex, both in function and in form. Speech is characterized by face to face communication; there is considerable repetition and redundancy and the listener has the opportunity to interrupt and seek clarification at any point. Writing transforms ephemeral speech into a permanent record. It is expected to be the expression of 'complete thoughts' which can be readily understood by readers removed by both time and space. And since there is the possibility of rereading a passage as many times as possible in order to understand the writer's intention, writing is considerably less redundant and repetitious than speech.

Speech and writing also differ in formal characteristics such as grammatical and textual structures and organization. Inevitably oral language forms will appear frequently in earlier attempts at writing. Kress (1982) points out that this is particularly true in the case of the sentence, for although the sentence is the basic unit in writing, speech is typically organized in terms of complexes of clauses. This realization may give teachers fresh insight where previously they struggled to understand why so many children have immense difficulty with the concept of sentence. Similarly, paragraphs, episodes and larger textual structures do not exist in speech and therefore have to be learned.

Developmental factors also need to be taken into account. Early writing is characterized by an almost exclusive use of co-ordinated main clauses *(I went to town and I bought a toy);* subordination *(When I went to town I bought a toy)* comes much later. Attempts to use more complex structures will often lead to grammatical and semantic errors (cf. Gannon & Czerniewska, 1980). Progress in learning to write involves taking risks and this in turn entails making mistakes. In this respect, learning to write is in no way different from any other learning activity.

All too often studies of writing have tended to concentrate on analyses of isolated pieces of children's work after they have been written. Our knowledge of writing as a process is thus extremely limited, and it is only recently that writers like Graves (1978) and Shaughnessy (1977) in America and Raban (1982), Richmond (1982a) and McLeod (1982a) in Britain have begun to explore precisely what is involved in a piece of writing, or how work progresses over a period of time. Research along these lines promises to be extremely useful and points already to some interesting conclusions.

A recurrent theme in the work of these writers is the information which can be gleaned from children's mistakes. In the same way that oral reading miscue analyses give an insight into how the child is learning to read, the most helpful approach to writing errors is to begin to ask *why* a child has produced a particular form rather than simply noting or correcting it. It is tempting to look upon departures from adult norms as shortcomings to be remedied at all costs. Such a view, however, overlooks the normal developmental progression in children's writing and the learning strategies which are constantly in operation. As Kress (op. cit.: 181-2) points out,

> What is at issue is a contest over convention, and while we may accept that the child's actions are unconventional in terms of society at large, his or her actions may have their own logic, consistency, coherence, and may indeed point towards possible alternative conventions.

Creativity and internal logic can be found in the writing of all children. However, these qualities are often highlighted in the work of second language learners. Take, for instance, the following story produced by Abdul, a 10 year old Pakistani boy who has been in England for a year:

I am wiating about my tarin sat
I have a toy tarin it go's on a ryyl. it go's very fast. it go's on elactarc and it his batans and the batans can be control. also you can control the tarin in any deracsan and olso you can put wood on top off the roof and it has a cemaney where the samke coms out. and runod the tarin there are plastc trees and plastc sattysun. dat all it has oh my toy

ABDUL

It might be tempting at first glance to dismiss this piece of writing as confused and hopeless, yet a closer look reveals some interesting patterns. Like many native speakers of his age, Abdul shows a monotonous use of *and* for joining sentences and does not attempt any kind of subordination. He does, however, have a clear idea of sentences and marks them off with a full stop in every case but one. On the other hand, he has no understanding that sentences start with a capital letter. Since his notion of sentence is so well-developed, this might be a profitable area for his teacher to draw attention to.

Most of the other technical difficulties relate to spelling mistakes. *Wiating, go's, his, olso, off* and *coms* are almost certainly misspellings. Various other words, however, give interesting indications of the sound patterns of his mother tongue. The insertion of a vowel between two consonants in t*a*rin, elact*a*rc, s*a*mke and s*a*ttysun would suggest that certain combinations of consonants are not permissible in his language. The use of *a* in s*a*t, el*a*ctarc, b*a*tans and der*a*acs*a*n would suggest that his vowel system does not coincide with that of English and that the *a* vowel has a wider distribution in Punjabi, which is in fact the case.

When seen in this light Abdul is clearly not a wild and hopeless guesser, but is applying himself intelligently to the task of spelling English words. Just as significant, there are only two mistakes which could reasonably be explained as second language learning errors in this piece of writing: *can be control* and *dat all it has*. In the final analysis, Abdul is a child who is making considerable progress and is showing a constructive and intelligent approach to the learning of another language.

Helpful strategies in teaching children to write

The exact mechanisms involved in learning to write are still very little understood, and it would seem that there is very little that children can be taught by way of explicit rules and exercises that will transform them into writers.

Certain approaches, however, appear to be more helpful than others. One of the recurring themes in discussions of writing is the battle between what has variously been called form and content, art and craft or transcription and composition. All writers have two separable but inter-related tasks. First they must formulate an idea, develop a sense of purpose and a sense of audience and find the appropriate words to achieve these ends. Then they must transcribe the composition, paying attention to spelling, punctuation and legibility. All too often these two aspects of writing compete for attention in children learning to write: the harder they try to approximate to accepted norms of transcription, the more the quality of their composition is likely to suffer: the more involved they are in composition, the untidier their presentation. We tend to forget that even adults produce scruffy first drafts! Ultimately composition and transcription must feed each other, but the realization that there are two processes involved in writing has important implications for both teachers and children. Although a 'good' piece of writing will reach acceptable levels in both composition and transcription, it is important, for instance, that the teacher should not dismiss or undervalue a piece of writing simply on the grounds that it is full of spelling mistakes and faulty punctuation. By the same token the child should be encouraged to separate the two processes and to look on rewriting and editing as integral elements of certain kinds of writing.

The distinction between transcription and composition emerges clearly in Raban's (1982) study, 'Influences on Children's Writing 5-9 years'. Close classroom observation and analysis of children's writing showed a positive relation between good pupil progress in transcription skills and teacher strategies such as: showing the children how to form letters and reading back what they had written, pointing to each word as they read it aloud; showing children where to start writing and marking the place; drawing children's attention to word-spacing and line-lengths; and providing the children with letter formation and individual word practice. Progress in composition, on the other hand, correlated positively with support in the following activities: teachers talking to the children about their drawings and encouraging them to include more of their thoughts in their pictures; asking them probing questions about their story prior to transcription; writing down exactly what each child said, reading the words aloud as they were written down; reading back the transcription for the child, pointing to each word and helping the child to do the same; helping the child to read back a completed tracing, copying, or writing, probing with interested questions to extend the composition; and reading aloud the final composition in the child's company.

Certain elements of transcription such as letter formation and word spacing can be helped by guided practice. Similarly, if we expect children to produce a particular kind of writing, such as an account of a science experiment or a résumé, their attention needs to be drawn to specific models. However, many other aspects of both transcription and composition can seldom be successfully taught. It would seem therefore that the most effective teacher strategy is to expose children to as wide a range of reading and writing as possible, in order to provide opportunities for them to spontaneously recognize and generalize from the patterns that they meet, and create an atmosphere in which children feel motivated to learn. Smith (1982:203-4), for instance, offers some summary statements which may help children in various aspects of writing:

Interest is developed by showing enthusiasm, providing demonstrations, by reading to children what they find interesting and by helping them to write what they feel interesting.

Sensitivity grows if children assume they can be writers and is destroyed if their expectations are demolished.

Handwriting is improved through practice that is not boring, allowing the child to write at a size and speed that is most comfortable but all the time working towards a reduction to conventional size and increase in speed. The best style and speed for composition will not be the best for neatness and legibility.

Spelling is fostered by providing spellings as they are required (to help the child), recognizing that spelling is primarily learned through reading and can be an obstacle to writing that children should be helped to overcome.

Punctuation is learned through reading and in use, when something a child has written or wants to write is conventionally punctuated. Children will not learn to punctuate if they are unable or afraid to write texts of sufficient complexity for punctuation to make a difference.

Grammar comes partly through 'correction' (*editing* would be a better word) when there is a desire to say something clearly, and partly through sensitivity in reading to written language that a child finds interesting and comprehensible.

Composition is learned in practice, when separated from the constraints of transcription, and stimulated by reading, discussion, and the opportunity for private reflection. Teachers contribute by helping children to improve and elaborate something of interest that the children have written or are trying to write.

Ideas develop from interaction and dialogue – with other people (adults and children), with books, films and drama, and especially with one's own writing. Ideas grow through exchange.

Fluency comes with increasing speed, confidence, and the avoidance of psychological blocks. The best springboard for writing still to come is writing already done.

Only-one-chance writing, such as examination essays, should be recognized as a special case requiring special practice. The skill comes with writing fluency and should not be permitted to interfere with the development of that fluency.

Neatness comes last, part of a final cleaning up if there is some purpose for it. Considerations of neatness should not slow down composition.

Richmond & McLeod (1981) develop a number of the ideas put forward by Smith in greater detail, with the older rather than the beginning writer in mind. They are concerned, in particular, with ways in which they can motivate children to widen the audience by writing for themselves and each other. This can be achieved in a number of ways. It is possible, for instance, to encourage collaboration in pairs, asking pupils to read each other's work in photocopy and make a note of anything which needs explanation, any changes in spelling or punctuation, any redundant or omitted words. Positive aspects of writing should also be stressed and children can be asked to draw attention to unusual words or to any part they think particularly good, as well as commenting on things they disagree with or want to know more about.

There are also possibilities for small group work. Children can be offered, for instance, different versions of a piece of writing by someone they don't know – maybe an older child who is an interesting writer. These pieces of work should be chosen, if possible, so that each one has notable weaknesses and strengths, and children should be asked to discuss these and try to understand the decisions that the writer has made.

Finally, the distribution and exhibition of writing should be as varied as possible. This can be achieved, Richmond and McLeod suggest, by:

> (i) covering the wall with exhibited writing, as well as pictures and posters, (ii) having a loose-leaf binder with transparent plastic leaves for putting writing in, one for each class, (iii) having a banda machine and an old typewriter in the room, (iv) going in for magazine production where the pupils do the donkeywork, not us, (v) making booklets of pupils' stories, poems and plays for distribution around the school, (vi) finding out-of-school audiences for pupils' work, when we can.

These suggestions, of course, apply equally to younger and to older pupils.

Second language learners and dialect speakers

All children learning to write face certain fundamental difficulties. Children for whom standard English is a second language or dialect, however, are confronted with additional problems. In some respects dialect speakers are at an even greater disadvantage than second language learners, since teachers are likely to make greater allowances for bilingual children. The special situation of many dialect speakers is summed up by Kress (1982:33) as follows:

> For some children the syntax of writing will be more familiar than for others, to whom it will be totally unfamiliar. Hence in a group of children some may start with knowledge which others have yet to acquire... .

Teachers are likely to attribute this difference in performance of children to differences in intelligence. There exists therefore an initial unnoticed hurdle in the learning of writing on which many children may stumble and never recover. They will not be fully competent writers and will be regarded as failures in the eyes of our literate society and in terms of our educational system.

Given the paucity of research on children's writing in general (cf. McLeod, 1982a), it is not surprising that very little work has been done on the writing of children for whom English is a second language. However, researchers like Lander (1979; undated), McLeod (1982a). Richmond (1979; 1982a), Studdert & Wiles (1982) and Wiles (1981) have made a promising start in this area and point to questions which merit a good deal more attention than they have previously received. Lander (1979), for instance, describes a study of children of West Indian origin. Results showed that the language of the West Indian group was further removed from standard English than that of British children of comparable background, though the differences between the groups were skewed to some extent by a small group of West Indian children who made a very large number of errors. Six statistically significant differences emerged, with the West Indian children producing the higher average number in each case. These were, in order of frequency of occurence,

  (i) lack of past tense marker (but he phone me twenty minutes ago)
 (ii) lack of plural marker (Simon saw smoke coming out of one of the boat)
(iii) lack of copula (it nice being on television)
(iv) preposition omitted (and drop a net him)
 (v) direct object omitted (he came down the stairs and hit and ran off)
(vi) unnecessary presence of preposition (Until he reached to Bond's Jaguar XJ6).

Five of these categories (i-iv; vi) can be explained in terms of the influence of West Indian Creoles, though the sixth (v) is more problematic and no explanation is offered.

Lander (undated) extends his study of writing to Pakistani children as well as children of West Indian origin and indigenous white pupils. He concludes that in writing both West Indians and Pakistanis use their own non-standard language and that these varieties are a good deal further removed from standard English than the language of indigenous whites. Results also indicate that the child's length of stay in Britain makes a difference in terms of distance from standard English; and that over 50 per cent of the significant differences between indigenous children and overseas children (features such as non-standard prepositions, the omission of plural markers and third person present singular markers) are common to all the overseas groups. Wiles (1981) and Studdert & Wiles (1982), however, go a step further. They suggest that it is impossible to be emphatic about the origin or cause of non-standard features in children's writing because all children, whatever their background, display on occasion such non-standard features.

'Interference' and 'Interlanguage'

In order to account for departures from standard English in the speech and writing of dialect and non-native speakers on the one hand, and similarities in these non-standard features across the groups on the other hand, it is helpful to look at two different theories of multilingual contact: 'linguistic interference' and 'interlanguage'.

The term interference comes to linguistics via psychology, though it originated in the study of the physical sciences. When we are engaged in a new learning activity we tend to carry over our experience from similar activities. Thus if we can already drive one make of car, there is a positive transfer when we start to drive another, since we carry over existing skills and knowledge to the new learning experience. If, however, a lever on the right of the steering wheel operates the windscreen wipers in one make and turns on the headlights in the other, it is quite possible that we will experience negative transfer – or interference – as for some time we turn on the headlights when in fact we want to start the windscreen wipers. In linguistics, writers such as Weinreich (1968) have postulated that interference takes place when speech habits which affect pronunciation, grammar and semantics are transferred by speakers from their first or dominant language to a second language.

Most of the discussion of interference in a British context has taken place around the subject of West Indian children and, although the concept remains perfectly respectable among linguists (cf. Newbrook, 1982), educationalists have often reacted very strongly against suggestions of dialect interference (cf. Wight, 1976; Goody, 1981). There would seem to be two main reasons for this reaction. The first was a widespread anxiety that linguistic interference might be used as a scapegoat in the discussion of West Indian underperformance, placing the blame firmly on the shoulders of the children themselves and diverting attention from institutional factors which were contributing to low achievement. For this reason, a cautious response to discussions of linguistic interference is certainly understandable.

The second reason would appear to have its roots in a linguistic accident. Interference in a technical sense is a purely descriptive label with no evaluative connotations. In everyday parlance, however, it has extremely negative associations. Richmond (1979) sums this up when he talks of the teacher who, having learned about dialect interference, goes back to the classroom to make sure that dialect will never interfere again! This is quite simply an unfortunate accident of the English language. French, for instance, makes a distinction between the technical *interférence* and the non-technical *brouiller/brouillage* (to interfere/interference). Many other languages make a similar distinction. In Germany and the Netherlands, where research into the educational situation of dialect speakers is considerably more advanced than in Britain, reference to dialect interference is completely uncontroversial and descriptions of the reactions of British educationalists are met with incredulity.

One of the consequences of the negative aura which seems to have grown up around interference is an unfortunate polarization. A. Rampton (1981), for instance, distinguishes three separate phases in the development of attitudes and approaches to West Indian language – linguistic deficit (which assumes that the language of West Indian children is inadequate for learning); linguistic interference (which claims that some West Indian children's language, though not inferior, is sufficiently different from standard English to cause difficulties); and the 'repertoires' approach (which values all languages and dialects as part of the child's linguistic repertoire). Yet although the first approach is incompatible with the last two, 'linguistic interference' and 'repertoires' are by no means mutually exclusive. The theoretical focus of much of my own early work, for instance, was on linguistic interference, whereas my discussion of the practical classroom implications of dialect diversity falls squarely under 'repertoires'. For this reason I can only agree with Riley (1982:8) when she suggests that the Rampton Committee is, at times, 'sadly adrift in its evaluation of research'.

The theory of interlanguage, as put forward by writers like Selinker (1972), takes the notion of linguistic interference one step further and, as such, has far greater explanatory possibilities, particularly in the case of second language learners. When speakers learn a new or target language they often fall short in various respects; attempts to produce the target language are known as interlanguage. But whereas writers like Lee (1968) proposed that interference is the *only* cause of 'errors', further studies have shown the situation to be far more complex. Selinker (op. cit.), for instance, proposes that one of at least five central psycholinguistic processes can give rise to error, including over-generalization and strategies of second language learning which result in a simplification of the target language.

Importantly, 'interlanguages' are seen as complete languages, rather than as restricted versions of another language – inasmuch as they are rule-governed, express meaning more or less adequately, and can be varied according to the situation.

The findings of Lander (1979: undated), Wiles (1981) and Studdert & Wiles (1982) that children from many different backgrounds make similar 'errors' are interesting in the light of this discussion. The fact that West Indian Creoles share many characteristics with the language of second language learners, for instance, leads Lander to suggest that perhaps these Creole features reflect basic language learning strategies, lending support to the theory of interlanguage which argues that creoles are the end product of universal cognitive processes of language learning (cf. Bickerton, 1981; Ladd & Edwards, 1982). It might be possible to extend this argument to English non-standard dialects, too, since many of the areas of variation in British dialects (cf. Chapter Five, pp.62-3) coincide with second language learning 'errors'.

Responses to dialect writing

What then are the prevailing attitudes towards non-standard features in children's writing? As was seen in the discussion of dialect diversity in Chapter Five we have travelled a long way from the position, held by Spens, Newbolt and other writers, that the moral wellbeing of society depended on the propagation of standard English. Innovators in this area have moved decisively in the direction of 'hospitality to diversity' (Levine, 1982), though it would seem that many of their more conservative colleagues remain to be persuaded of the logic of such a step.

McLeod (1982b), for instance, refers to the now almost official litany that 'schools should value the language which all children, including West Indians, bring to school', but suspects that this phrase is 'now uttered much more than it is understood and very very much more often than it is implemented'. Studdert & Wiles (1982) make a similar point and show the ways in which language policies vary enormously from school to school and often seem to contradict each other within the same school:

> Some schools, for example, may accept and even encourage the use of dialect in speech (role play, drama, etc.) but have a school language policy which urges the use of standard English in writing. It is not unknown for schools to state that they will not display writing in dialect on the classroom walls. Other schools may even encourage the use of dialect in writing, particularly for dialogue or perhaps poetry. What teachers find less acceptable is the combination of the two, perhaps because it is difficult to respond to: Is it right or wrong? How do I mark it?

One thing remains clear: there is a strong association in people's minds between non-standard features and poor quality writing. Lander (1981), for instance, shows how poor stories were generally judged to be more non-standard than good stories, although this was not necessarily the case. And when stories were *perceived* by the subject as using non-standard language, they were regularly assessed less favourably than stories perceived as using the standard. Cheshire (1982a) demonstrates the ways in which English working class children consistently use fewer dialect features in writing than in speech. This sensitivity to situation, however, is usually overlooked: we tend to notice the non-standard features to the exclusion of the standard.

Careful analysis of children's writing is required to overcome bias of this kind. All too often we judge a piece of writing far more superficially than it deserves, and technical weakness tends to distract our attention from the actual content. Teachers also tend to react overzealously to dialect features in children's writing. They feel it is negligent and unfair to allow them to pass without comment and yet 'correctness' will inevitably be selective, partly because it is too enormous a task to 'correct' everything and partly because teachers rightly understand that such a strategy would be demoralizing for the child. Take this example of a teacher's response to a piece of writing by an 11 year old Reading child, from Cheshire (1982a):

> Last Christmas Eve Mum and Dad was out round the pub drinking. There was me, Pam, my sister and brother Bob at home watching TV. We w̄as in bed about one hour when Mum and Dad <u>was</u> coming up to bed then so we went to sleep. In the morning we got up and there <u>was</u> all our presents on the tree.

'Was' is used consistently throughout this passage, yet the teacher ignores the first two instances, puts a cross above the third, but does not supply the standard form, and underlines the fourth and fifth, writing in 'were' above them. Such a strategy is unlikely to communicate to the child that the appropriate past tense form of the verb 'to be' when the subject is plural is 'were' and not 'was' in standard English. There is evidence of hypercorrection in both West Indian and British children's writing which may well be due in part at least to inconsistency in teacher marking. Examples from West Indian children, such as:

> The *slides makes* the sugar *canes turns* into the box.

suggest something far more than carelessness or 'slips of the pen'. It seems very likely that the child has been corrected so often for leaving *s* off plurals and present tense verbs that he has decided to over-compensate and add an *s* whenever he is in doubt.

Much of the retention of dialect features in both speech and writing can almost certainly be explained in terms of the very close relationship between language and identity. The teacher who constantly critizes and 'corrects' may well be perceived as rejecting the dialect speaker's culture and values. And it is important to remember that the child's own community, in particular the peer group, exercises far more powerful control over the child's language than the teacher.

So what, then, is the alternative? Most teachers would be appalled at the idea of not correcting children's work. The question of dialect difference, however, needs to be seen in perspective. Consider the following piece of writing by Julie, a 14 year old Reading girl, in terms of, on the one hand, errors, which arise from the technical aspects of writing (such as spelling and punctuation) and, on the other hand, actual dialect features.

<u>Jane</u>

Jane is a girl ~~who~~ who, is very Rich[1/2] She Lives[3] With[4] her grane[5] and granedad[6/7] and her two uncoles[8] and her two Anuties[9/10] they own a big Ranch[11] and a big Manchen.[12] Jane has meet[13] this[d] Boy Cald[14] Mitch[15] he is not Rich[16] he Lives[17] in a Flate[18] at a Colege. he is[19] practersine[20] Law. Jane and Mitch has planed[21] to get Married in a Months time. Jane's grane[22] and granedad[23] are trying to put her off becaue she is youst[24] to haveing[25] every thinck[26] She ever wants. Well[27] the month was up and.[28] Jane and Mitch got Married[29] She moved out fouth[30] and the Manchen[31] and moved in to the flate[32] with Mitch. She was in town one day and she see[c] a fur Coat[33] She went strat[34] home and told Mitch about the coat and Mitch Said that she cud[35] not have it. She Left him and went back to her grane[36] and grandad and she got the fur Coat. So being Rich[37] and Spialed[38] Dont[39/d] bring happy Ness[40]

By Julie

Errors

1 Rich/rich
2 Omission of full stop
3 Lives/lives
4 With/with
5 grane/gran
6 granedad/grandad
7 Unnecessary full stop
8 uncoles/uncles
9 Anuties/aunties
10 Omission of full stop leading to non-use of capital in following word
11 Ranch/ranch
12 Manchen/mansion
13 Boy/boy
14 cald/called
15 Omission of full stop leading to non-use of capital in following word
16 Omission of full stop leading to non-use of capital in following word
17 Live's/lives
18 flate/flat
19 he/He
20 practersine/practising
21 planed/planned
22 grane/gran
23 granedad/grandad
24 youst/used
25 haveing/having
26 every think/everything
27 Omission of comma
28 Unnecessary full stop
29 Omission of full stop leading to non-use of capital in following word
30 Fourthhand/forthwith? preposition *from* omitted?
31 manchen/mansion
32 flate/flat
33 Omission of full stop leading to non-use of capital in following word
34 strat/straight
35 cud/could
36 grane/gran
37 Rich/rich
38 spialed/spoiled
39 Don't/don't
40 happy Ness/happiness

Dialect features

a has meet – has met
b has planned – have planned
c She see – she saw
d don't bring – doesn't bring

This analysis (based on Richmond, 1979) makes it clear that 'errors' are a far more serious problem in Julie's writing than dialect features: they number 40 while there are only four dialect features. Two of the 'errors' (8: 'uncoles' and 26: 'every think') show the influence of dialect pronunciation on spelling. They have not, however, been assigned to the column for dialect features because the mismatch between spelling and pronunciation can be considerable for standard and dialect speakers alike, and no one group has an advantage over any others in this respect. Rules for spelling are thus an accepted part of the conventions for writing, and misspellings are best treated as technical mistakes whether or not they are dialect-based. Nonetheless a knowledge of differences in pronunciation is obviously useful if teachers are to understand how a child arrives at a particular spelling.

There can be no hard and fast rules for responding to dialect in children's writing. The needs of the individual clearly have to be taken into consideration and whereas some children would be hurt and confused if dialect features were pointed out, others might well be angry if they were not. Allowance also needs to be made for children's stages of development: the first school child dictating a 'story' to the teacher is likely to be bewildered by attempts to translate dialect forms into the standard, whereas the child in an examination class will suffer if attention is not drawn to inadvertent use of dialect. In the majority of cases, however, it would seem more prudent to concentrate on the technical aspects of writing, leaving dialect features alone, at least until the last few years of school. By this point many dialect features will have been edited out spontaneously. More important, it is possible to explain clearly and systematically the differences which exist to children who are likely at this stage to be more motivated in terms of exam success than are younger pupils. Many teachers and parents feel alarmed by this suggestion and think it is in the best interest of the children that all aspects of their work should be 'corrected'. It should be remembered, however, that technical difficulties with organization, punctuation and spelling are a far more serious problem in children's writing than are dialect features. It should also be remembered that the selective marking strategies which many teachers currently employ may well result in confusion and linguistic insecurity on the part of the child.

Response to bilingual children's writing

A similar approach would seem to be called for in the case of children for whom English is a second language. Undue attention to form at the expense of content can be both short-sighted and counterproductive. Children progress unevenly and at their own pace towards the target language and the only effect which correction of all the second language learning errors in a piece of writing is likely to achieve is confusion and demoralization. A more positive response would seem to lie in the noting and monitoring – for the teacher's benefit – of recurring errors, and in evaluating children's writing by wider criteria than simply its nearness to standard English. Studdert & Wiles (1982) exemplify such an approach, giving examples of the range of writing which teachers are likely to encounter in the multilingual classroom and suggesting the most appropriate response. Take, for instance, their analysis of a story written by Siu-Ching, a second year junior child:

Siu-Ching's Story
 1 The farmer saw a palace with gold roof and he ask the sold is my
 2 daughter in there and the soldier laugh and one of the soldier
 3 said your daughter in here and the farmer said yes she got
 4 married with the king of the crocodile and the farmer daughter
 5 came out of the palace and the farmer daughter was so happy to
 6 see her Father and the farmer was so happy and them the
 7 crocodiles came and he said your daughter is my wife and the farmer
 8 said no it is not your wife and the crocodile said I married your
 9 daughter and them the farmer daughter said I hate crocodiles and the
10 farmer said I going to take my daughter home and the crocodiles said
11 your not going to take her home and then the farmer daughter said oh yes
12 he is going to take me home and the farmer took her daughter home
13 and the farmer wife are so glad to see her daughter and they all have
14 dinner and them she went out to play in the garden and soon it was
15 bed time for the farmers daughter in the morning she had her breakfast
16 when the farmer daughter finish her break fast and then the farme
17 daughter was going to the palace to see the crocodiles and them she
18 saw the crocodiles and she run home to talk to her Father.

Comments
Probably the first thing that one would want to say about Siu-Ching's story is that it shows clearly that she has responded enthusiastically to the task that has been set. This extended piece of writing indicates that she has understood the dilemma facing the farmer's daughter and wants to find a way of resolving this unnatural situation. At the same time she realises that it is a fairy tale and the end of her story has the daughter hovering uneasily between the two worlds. Siu-Ching is still working her way towards standard English but this in no ways deters her from embarking on quite a long piece of writing. This is a most encouraging aspect of the work.

   The most striking feature of the writing is the total lack of punctuation. But it is not as difficult to read as one might imagine for the frequent use of 'and' serves to mark progressive stages in the story line. Siu-Ching clearly needs a lot of help with punctuation. She needs to learn how to mark sentence boundaries. A related but more complex task will be that of learning how to indicate direct speech within the narrative. She will also need to be encouraged to vary her sentence patterns so that the story line can be carried forward without continual reliance on the 'and then' pattern, but this could well be seen as an issue to be tackled later. These of course are issues for all children and persist well into the secondary school as many teachers of older children have indicated. Because such features are widespread in the writing of all children they cannot be seen as directly related to the fact that Siu-Ching's mother tongue is Cantonese. But some of the language Siu-Ching uses does seem to indicate a lack of familiarity with certain English usage.

Turning to the language itself we notice the following categories of 'error':

1. *omissions*

(a) *the indefinite article* in line 1, 'with gold roof'. Probably just a slip as we frequently jump over words in our haste to write or speak on.

(b) *the auxiliary* in line 10, 'I going to take...'. Probably also a slip as Siu-Ching uses the auxiliary correctly on several occasions in her story.

(c) *possessive 's'* On six occasions Siu-Ching has written 'the farmer daughter' instead of 'the farmer's daughter'. Only once does she add the 's' to mark possession. This does indicate lack of familiarity with the formation of the possessive in English. It might well be worth considering how Siu-Ching's attention can be drawn to this feature - through the presentation of clear models (speech and writing) or maybe through a game where possession is an important element, (e.g., a 'happy families' type of activity).

(d) *plural 's'* On two out of six occasions Siu-Ching omits the 's' required to mark a plural noun (e.g., 'crocodile' instead of 'crocodiles'). As she gets it right most of the time it is probably not worth highlighting this error but the teacher will possibly want to be on the look out for it in future pieces of writing in case it should become a persistent feature.

2. *formation of past tense*

Although there are six errors in this category which tend to stand out as one reads the story, it is important to note that on a further 18 occasions Siu-Ching has used the past tense correctly. On three occasions she has omitted the regular past tense marker 'ed'. There is only one instance of her using this form correctly (married) so her teacher might feel it appropriate to discuss this aspect of English with her. Again it would be important to check by reference to other pieces of writing that it really is a persistent feature.

The 'are' and 'have' in line 13 which should have been 'was' and 'had' are possibly due to confusion with the time sequence of the story. Children are frequently inconsistent in their use of tenses when writing stories (does the use of the historic present in many stories for young children also contribute to this confusion?). In any case Siu-Ching knows the forms 'was' and 'had' as she uses them correctly in other parts of the story.

The 'run' for 'ran' in the final line could be lack of knowledge of this irregular past tense form but it could equally be a learnt London feature as many of the mother tongue English children use it in their stories also.

The reasons why Siu-Ching has used these six non-standard forms are not at all clear cut. The correct formation of the past tense is something that takes all children a long time to sort out. Consider the number of 'runned', 'sended' and 'eated' etc. forms that we meet even at the top of the junior school. Siu-Ching has no examples of this particular developmental feature in this story but many examples occur in the stories of other children.

3. *pronominal confusion/substitution*

On two occasions Siu-Ching uses the wrong pronouns - the farmer took her daughter home' and 'it is not your wife'. This is quite possibly due to the fact that in Cantonese there is one pronoun for all three genders so this is an aspect of English with which Siu-Ching may need extra support. However most of the time in this story she gets it right so it would be unwise to start focusing on this feature without a good deal more evidence of serious confusion.

It is worth pointing out that all the above features, omissions of various kinds, incorrect formation of the past tense and different pronominal usage, are said to be commonly found in the language of children of Caribbean origin. If Siu-Ching or her parents had come from the West Indies these would have been seen as evidence of dialect interference. Once again it is obvious that there are no clear-cut linguistic boundaries between children with different language backgrounds.

One further small feature in Siu-Ching's writing which doesn't quite sound English is the expression 'to get married with'. 'Married to' is the form normally found. The use of correct prepositions and adverbial particles is notoriously difficult in English and even mother tongue English speakers take a long time to learn and use appropriately all the colloquial expressions formed by a verb+preposition/adverb. Siu-Ching will learn to use these expressions appropriately as she meets and practises more examples.

Siu-Ching needs help with a good many aspects of her writing, but to tackle them all at once would be counterproductive. She is making a very creditable attempt at writing in a second language and needs every encouragement to go on writing with the obvious enthusiasm that she displays here. Her teacher will probably find it helpful to present her with plenty of good story models, concentrate on the organisational aspects of her writing and monitor her English usage to check that it continues to approximate to acceptable school English.

Opportunities for writing in other languages and dialects

The preponderance of standard English literature in British schools means that speakers of English as a second language and dialect speaking children have a serious shortage of written models. The growth of interest in mother tongue teaching and the increased awareness of many librarians is going some way towards remedying the dearth of material available in other languages. There has also been an increase in the quantity of dialect literature suitable for schools. Various community writing projects such as Centerprise, the Commonplace Workshop and the Peckham Publishing Project produce some publications in dialect. The ILEA Learning Materials Service also includes some dialect material in both book and cassette form. Ultimately, however, the burden of responsibility lies with the school and most non-standard writing will be produced by the children themselves.

There are many advantages in encouraging children to write in another language or dialect. It may simply be more appropriate when handling a particular theme to use the form of language normally associated with it. Paul George's *Memories,* an ILEA publication which recounts his life in Grenada before coming to England, would lose much of its warmth and immediacy if it were written in standard English. By the same token, it is inconceivable that the anger at white society which permeates the work of Linton Kwesi Johnson could be conveyed by anything other than Jamaican Creole. Writing may also be easier and more natural in a language or dialect in which you feel more comfortable. *Jennifer* and *Brixton Blues* (Richmond, 1978), *Thursday Afternoons* (see Chapter Six) and many other successful examples of children's writing, have been produced by children often labelled 'remedial' or 'disruptive' in more conventional settings.

Teachers tend to shy away from allowing children to write in languages or dialects they do not understand themselves. In doing so they deny their pupils the opportunity to demonstrate valuable skills, and to develop their ability as translators as they explain the content of their writing to friends and teachers. The kind of situation which readily gives rise to writing of this kind can be illustrated by the experience of Audrey Gregory, a Reading teacher working with a group of bilingual children on the theme of games. Snakes recurred as a topic of conversation as children worked on variants of Snakes and Ladders: for many, they had been part of daily life before coming to England. Volunteers recorded their stories in their mother tongue and then translated the stories for the benefit of the teacher and other children who did not speak their language. It was a natural progression to write the stories in Urdu and English as Javed Akram does below.

بسم الله الرحمن الرحیم

بڑا زبردست سانپ

مجھے یاد ہے جب میں آزاد کشمیر میں رہتا تھا ایک دن میں نے ایک بڑا
سانپ دیکھا وہ سانپ ہمارے گھوں میں تھا۔ وہ سانپ جھومتا ہوا دریا
کی طرف پانی پینے کے لیے جا رہا اس دن کی بات ہے جب میں پینے چاچا کے ساتھ
گائیں کو کے کر دریا پر انہیں پانی پلانے کے لیے وہاں لے جاتے ہیں۔ اور ہم
گائیں کو دریا دھوتے بھی ہیں پھر ہاں پیر بڑی دھوپ تھی سو سج جک رہا تھا۔
ہم آپس کی گائیں کو اس دن دھوتے ہیں اس دن دھوب چمک رہی ہو۔
یہاں بہت سے آدمی گائیں کو دھوتے تھے ہیں کیونکہ اس دن جمعہ ہوتا ہے۔
یا کہان میں ہر جمعہ کو دیاں پیر بھٹی ہوتی ہے کوئی آدمی کام پر اور اسکول
کے بچے اسکول نہیں جاتے۔ اور لوگوں نے اپنے بچوں کو گائیں پکڑ اکر سانپ
کو مارنے کے لیے چلے گئے ایک آدمی تھا جو اچھا سانتانا لگا سکتا تھا۔ اس نے سانپ
پیچھڑا مارا اور دردن سانپ مرگیا۔ اسی آدمی نے پھر پھڑ مارا کے سانپ کے بالکل
مرجائے۔

جاوید اکرم   Javed Akram

A big dangerous snake

I remember when I lived in Azad
Kashmir one day I saw a snake in the
village. he was wriggling away to drink
some water in the river It happened when
I was going to the river with my uncle
to take the bulls to drink water. We were
also going to take them in the river to wash
them It was a sunny day We usually
washed the bulls on a sunny day There
were a lot of people near the river washing
their bulls because It was Friday in azad kashmir
Friday is a holiday nobody goes to school or to
work. then The fathers and the uncles told the
children to hold the bulls. Then the men went to
try to kill the snake one of the men who was
good at throwing a knife, Throw his knife at the
snake. It hit the snake, in its throat and killed
It Then he hit It again to make sure the snake
was dead

The AND

The opportunity to draw on different language backgrounds should, of course, be an unselfconscious option open to children and never imposed by the teacher. Ways in which children can be motivated to learn and possibilities for widening the audience beyond the teacher have already been outlined above. There is every reason why classroom displays, class books, school magazines and other efforts should go beyond teacher-edited standard English texts to include material in other languages. Magazines, for instance, provide unlimited opportunities for drawing on the whole range of linguistic skills of children in the school, particularly when contributors are encouraged to write for themselves and each other rather than an adult audience. Redlands Magazine, produced by Redlands Primary School, Reading, is an excellent example of interesting and varied writing from children of many different social, ethnic and linguistic backgrounds and also from a broad age range. Young children tend to write about their personal experiences (see p.132). Older children provide tongue twisters, jokes, book reviews, poems, recipes, news items and, in some cases, contributions in their own languages (see p.133).

Summary
Writing presents similar problems for all children. It involves the mastery of transcription and composition skills and draws on structures and organization which often differ in significant ways from speech. The processes by which we learn to write are still little understood, but the most helpful teacher response would seem to be to expose children to as wide a range as possible of enjoyable reading and writing experiences which will allow them to recognize and generalize from patterns for themselves. Creativity and internal logic are apparent in the writing of all children and should be recognized as such rather than as indications of weakness or low intelligence.

Children who speak a language or dialect other than standard English face additional problems through the lack of awareness of teachers. Constant attempts to 'correct' non-standard forms are likely to be counterproductive: they may well give rise to hypercorrection and feelings of inadequacy which are hardly conducive to confident writing. All children should be given the opportunity to explore themes which they find interesting. For many, it may be either easier or more natural to write about a given theme in a language or dialect other than standard English. Support for initiatives of this kind does not detract from the educational goal of producing children who are literate in standard English. Such a goal

My sister and my brother
went on on aeroplane They
went to Pakistan

Fozia

La mia amica in Italia
si chiame Cristianna

Laura

I CRY when I have a bad dream.

Jason

depends on children who have a well-developed sense of themselves as writers. Attempts to draw on their linguistic skills are likely to contribute to this sense; the devaluation of their skills is likely to produce the opposite effect.

میرا نام آمثان یونس ہے ۔

میں سکول جاتی ہوں ۔

میری دو بہنیں ہیں ۔

ایک کا نام اجمہ ہے اور دوسری کا نام انوار ہے ۔

اجمہ مجھ سے بڑی ہے اور انوار چھوٹی ہے ۔

Afshan

Can you count in Punjabi?

1	2	3	4	5
ek	do	tin	char	panj

6	7	8	9	10
chey	sat	at	no	das.

Satwant

Further reading and resources

Chapter One

Useful introductions to the subject of language in education are contained in Trudgill (1975) *Accent, Dialect and the School* and Stubbs (1976) *Language, Schools and Classrooms*. The most comprehensive coverage of this area to date, however, is contained in John Edwards (1979b) *Language and Disadvantage*. N. Mercer (ed.) (1981) *Language in School and Community* is another useful volume, combining as it does theoretical and practical considerations.

Attitudes towards language in general are discussed in Giles & Powesland (1975) *Speech Style and Social Evaluation* and Ryan & Giles (1982) *Attitudes towards Language Variation: Social and Applied Contexts*.

Chapter Two

The fullest and most relevant discussion of linguistic diversity in an educational setting to date is to be found in Rosen & Burgess (1980) *Languages and Dialects of London School Children*. The report of the Linguistic Minorities Project team, *The Other Languages of England* (provisional title) due to be published in 1984, will, however, considerably supplement our knowledge of this area. A fuller discussion of the policy aspects of teaching English as a second language is contained in V. Edwards (1984) 'Language Policy in Multicultural Britain'. The teachers' book of the Schools Council project in English for immigrant children, *Scope* Stage 1 (2nd edition, Longman, 1978), provides guidance on the methodology of teaching English as a second language to small groups, while Hester, Wainwright & Fraser (1977) *English as a Second Language in Multiracial Schools* offers a useful annotated bibliography describing books and materials available to support second language 'learning. Brown (1979) *Mother Tongue to English* deals specifically with the situation of young bilingual children.

The 'Language in the Multiethnic Primary School' video-cassettes are available for hire or sale to ILEA teachers from the Learning

Materials Service, Publishing Centre, Highbury, Station Road, London N1 15B; and by teachers outside ILEA from the Central Film Library, Chalfont Grove, Gerrards Cross, Bucks SL9 8TN. ILEA also produces 'The First Few Weeks', booklets designed to be used by teachers, parents and children, providing vocabulary for coping with day to day communication in Chinese, Gujarati, Punjabi and Urdu in conjunction with English (available from the Learning Materials Service Publishing Centre).

Further information on the SLIPP project is available from the Centre for Urban Educational Studies, Robert Montefiore School Building, Underwood Road, London E1 5AD.

The Centre for Information on Language Teaching and Research (CILT), 20 Carlton House Terrace, London SW1 5AP, produces a wide range of publications and bibliographies relevant to the teaching of English as a second language.

Chapter Three

A concise but thorough overview of the issues involved in Mother Tongue Teaching is to be found in *Issues in Race and Education*, no. 35. Chapter 12 of Twitchin & Demuth *Multicultural Education* also provides a useful introduction to this area. The fullest discussion of bilingual education in a British context has been prepared by John Wright: *Bilingualism in Education* is available from Issues in Race and Education, 11 Carleton Gardens, London N19 5AQ. The most comprehensive source of information on Mother Tongue teaching on a local and national level is the National Committee for Mother Tongue Teaching (NCMTT), 5 Musgrave Crescent, London SW6.

Various schools broadcasts have made use of mother tongues from a number of countries, including 'You and Me' which has produced stories in seven languages and English in both book and cassette form. Details are available from BBC Cleveland, 99 Linthorpe Road, Middlesbrough, Cleveland.

The CRE (Elliot House, 10-12 Allington Street, London SW1E 5EH) provides the free leaflets *Books and Periodicals in Asian Languages* and the *Ethnic Minority Press*. Clough & Quarmby (1979) *A Public Library Service for Ethnic Minorities in Great Britain* contains information on specialized library services, publishers and booksellers.

Further information on the BUF project is available from the Centre for Urban Educational Studies, Robert Montefiore School Building, Underwood Road, London E1 5AD. 'Face Play' is available from the Learning Materials Service Publishing Centre for ILEA teachers and from ESA Creative Learning Ltd., Fairview Road,

Stevenage, Hertfordshire SG1 2NX for teachers outside ILEA. 'Working with Young Bilingual Children' videocassettes can be obtained from the Learning Materials Service by ILEA teachers and from the Central Film Library by other teachers (see notes on Chapter Two for full details).

Chapter Four

Fuller treatment of the language of the British Black community is contained in V. Edwards (1979) *The West Indian Language Issue in British Schools* and Sutcliffe (1982) *British Black English.* The most recent overview of research in this area is to be found in V. Edwards (1981) 'Black British English: A Bibliographical Essay on the Language of Children of West Indian Origin' in *Sage Race Relations Abstracts* 5 (384): 1-26. It is hoped that the SSRC funded project 'Patterns of language use in British Black adolescents', jointly directed by Viv Edwards and David Sutcliffe and starting in January 1983, will go at least some way towards remedying the serious gaps in our knowledge of this area.

Chapter Five

Trudgill (1974a) *Sociolinguistics* is an excellent introduction to this general area. More detailed and technical accounts are to be found in Trudgill (1974) *The Social Differentiation of English in Norwich,* Macaulay (1977) *Language, Social Class and Education: a Glasgow Study,* Milroy (1980) *Language and Social Networks* (based on a study of Belfast speech), Heath (1980) *The Pronunciation of English in Cannock, Staffordshire* and Cheshire (1982b) *Variation in a British Dialect: a Socio-linguistic Study* (based on Reading speech). Useful overviews of this area are contained in Trudgill (1978) *Sociolinguistic Patterns in British English,* Hughes & Trudgill (1979) *English Accents and Dialects* and Trudgill (1983) *Language in the British Isles.* Various more popularized accounts of British regional speech are also available, including the following:

BUCKINGHAMSHIRE
Buckinghamshire Dialect, H. Harman. East Ardsley: SR Publishers, 1970.
CHESHIRE
Cheshire Chatter, P. Wright. Clapham, N. Yorks: Dalesman Books, 1974.
COCKNEY
A Load of Cockney Cobblers, B. Aylwin. Edinburgh: Johnston and Bacon, 1973.

The Cockney: a Survey of London Life and Language, J. Franklyn. London: Andre Deutsch, 1953.

Cockney Past and Present, J. Matthews. London: Routledge & Kegan Paul, 1938, reprinted 1972.

Cockney Dialect and Slang, P. Wright. London: Batsford, 1981.

CUMBRIA

Cumbrian Dialect, P. Wright. Clapham, N. Yorks: Dalesman Books, 1979.

Cumbrian Chat, P. Wright, Clapham, N. Yorks: Dalesman Books, not dated.

DERBYSHIRE

Derbyshire Drawl, P. Wright. Clapham, N. Yorks: Dalesman Books, 1975.

GEORDIE

Larn Yersel Geordie, S. Dobson. Newcastle-upon-Tyne: Frank Graham, 1976.

HEREFORDSHIRE

Herefordshire Speech, W. Leeds. Pound Cottage, Upton Crews, Ross-on-Wye: the author.

LANCASHIRE

Lanky Twang, P. Wright. Clapham, N. Yorks: Dalesman Books, 1972.

Lancashire Dialect, P. Wright. Clapham, N. Yorks: Dalesman Books, 1976.

LINCOLNSHIRE

Lincolnshire Dialects, G. Campion. Boston, Lincs: Richard Kay, 1976.

LIVERPOOL

Lern Yerself Scouse: How to Talk Proper in Liverpool, F. Shaw, F. Spiegl & S. Kelly. Liverpool: Scouse Press, 1966.

Lern Yerself Scouse—or the ABC of Scouse, Vol. 2, F. Spiegl. Liverpool: Scouse Press, 1979.

NORFOLK

Broad Norfolk, J. Mardle, Norwich: Wensum Books, 1973.

NOTTINGHAM

Notts Natter, P. Wright. Clapham, N. Yorks: Dalesman Books, not dated.

SCOTS ENGLISH

Talking Glasgow, A. Mackie. Belfast: Blackstaff, 1978.

Speak Scotch or Whistle, A. Mackie. Belfast: Blackstaff, 1979.

SOUTH-WEST ENGLAND

Krek Waiter's Peak Bristle: A Guide to What the Natives Say and Mean in the Heart of Wess Vinglum, D. Robson. Bristol: Abson Press, 1970.

Son of Bristle: A Second Guide to What the Natives Say and Mean in the Heart of Wess Vinglum, D. Robson. Bristol: Abson Press, 1971.

Wessex Dialect, N. Rogers. Bradford-on-Avon: Moonraker Press, 1979.

SUFFOLK

Suffolk Dialect, A. Claxton. Woodbridge, Suffolk: Boydell Press, 1981.

YORKSHIRE

Teach thissen tyke, A Mitchell & S. Waddell. Newcastle-upon-Tyne: Graham, 1971.

Yorkshire Yammer, P. Wright. Clapham, N. Yorks: Dalesman Books, 1973.

This chapter (and also Chapter Eight) draws heavily at points on the insights and experience of John Richmond. His work is now most easily accessible in *The Resources of Classroom Language* (Edward Arnold, 1982) and *Investigating Our Language,* co-authored with Helen Savva (Edward Arnold, 1983).

For full details of 'Language in the Multiethnic primary school' videocassettes, see notes on Chapter Two.

Chapter Six

The examples which have been chosen to illustrate the potential of building on children's talk in this chapter have necessarily been selective. Two further areas which draw heavily on children's interests and expertise, and which would have been included had space allowed, are music and games. The reader is strongly recommended to consult two very useful accounts by classroom practitioners of work undertaken around these themes. The first concentrates on games and is contained in a special issue of *Child Education,* July 1982, compiled by Audrey Gregory, Norah Wollard, Jill Bennett and Wyn Brooks. The second 'Music in the Classroom' by Steve Hoyle, is to be found in the CRE *Education Journal* IV(1). Vulliamy & Lee (1980) *Pop Music in School* is also a very useful resource for teachers interested in the potential of music for language work.

Children, Language and Literature is an in-service pack for teachers, from the Open University, which includes a cassette recording of oral literature created and performed by children from Brixton, and children's playground rhymes.

Thursday Afternoons: Stories and Poems can be obtained from Slough Teachers' Centre, Wexham Road, Slough. Another very useful publication from Berkshire teachers is *Talking and Telling,* articles and examples of children's work built around story telling activities. It is available from the English Language Centre, Lydford Road, Reading, Berkshire.

Chapter Seven

The most comprehensive accounts of the theoretical foundations of reading are to be found in Frank Smith (1978) *Reading* and *Language and Literacy: the Selected Writings of K. S. Goodman* (Gollasch, 1982). Books which combine a theoretical background with practical suggestions for the teacher include Moon & Raban (1980) *A Question of Reading,* Southgate et al. (1981) *Extending Beginning Reading* and Arnold (1982) *Listening to Children Reading.* The Natty Dread Stories referred to in this chapter are available from Dread Beat Publications, 84 Rattray Road, London SW2. Bookshops which specialize in books by Afro-Caribbean, British Black and Asian writers include:

Grass Roots Storefront
61 Goldbourne Road
London W10

Harriet Tubman Bookshop
27-29 Grove Lane
Handsworth
Birmingham

Hindi Book Centre
(books in Hindi, Urdu, Punjabi, Gujarati and Bengali)
69 Great Russell Street
London WC1B 3BQ

Independent Publishing Company (Soma Bookshop)
38 Kennington Lane
London SE11 4LS

New Beacon Books
76 Stroud Green Road
London N4 3EN

Sabarr Books
378 Coldharbour Lane
London SW9

Shakti Bookhouse
46 High Street
Southall
Middlesex

Third World Publications
152 Stratford Road
Birmingham B11 1RD

Walter Rodney Bookshop
(run by Bogle L'Ouverture Publications)
5a Chignell Place
Ealing
London W13 0TJ.

Chapter Eight

Kress (1982) *Learning to Write* and Frank Smith (1982) *Writing and the Writer* provide perhaps the fullest discussions to date on how children learn to write and the writing process. A useful developmental perspective on children's writing is contained in Gannon & Czerniewska (1980) *Using Linguistics: an Educational Focus.* The ILEA *English Magazine* often provides very useful discussions of children's writing with a practical bias (see, for example, issues no. 6, 'Writing in School', no. 8, 'Writing… Curriculum', and no. 9, 'Writing …Gender'. Comunity publishing projects which encourage writing by working class young people and adults include:

Black Ink Collective
1 Gresham Road
London SW9

Centerprise
136 Kingsland High Street
London E8

The Commonplace Workshop
73 Balfour Street
London SE17

Peckham Publishing Project
The Bookplace
13 Peckham High Street
London SE15

The ILEA English Centre, Ebury Teachers' Centre, Sutherland Steet, London SW1 has also been responsible for publishing a wide range of very useful material, including *Our Lives,* a collection of 11 autobiographical stories by young people. The following stories from *Our Lives* are also available separately: *Small Accidents,* Sabir Bandali's account of his childhood in Uganda, arrival in England and family life in Tooting; *In the Melting Pot,* Chelsea Herbert's lively story written in Jamaican Creole about a girl who lives in Paddington and the boy who moves in next door; *Jamaica Child,* an account of childhood in Jamaica by Errol O'Conner; and *My Life,* an account of life in Morocco by Mohammed Elbaja.

References

ARNOLD, H. (1982), *Listening to Children Reading,* Hodder & Stoughton.

ASSOCIATION OF TEACHERS OF ENGLISH TO PUPILS FROM OVERSEAS (ATEPO) (Birmingham Branch) (1970), *Work Group of West Indian Pupils Report.*

BAILEY, B. L. (1966), *A Transformational Grammar of Jamaican Creole,* Cambridge University Press.

BAKHSH, Q. & WALKER, N. (1980), *Unrealised Potential. Gravesend Study: A Case for Additional Resources under Section II,* Gravesend & District Community Relations Council.

BARNES, D., BRITTON, J. & ROSEN, H. (1969), *Language, the Learner and the School,* Penguin.

BARNES, D. (1976), *From Communication to Curriculum.* Penguin.

BARRERA-VASQUEZ, A. (1963), 'The Tarascan Project in Mexico', in UNESCO (ed.), *The Use of Vernacular Languages in Education,* Paris: UNESCO.

BELL, R. (1978), 'Bilingualism in Lancaster. A pilot study of attitudes and usage', Dept of Linguistics, Lancaster University.

BELLIN, W. (1980), 'The EEC Directive on the Education of the Children of Migrant Workers: a comparison of the Commission's proposed directive and the Council directive together with a parallel text', *Polyglot* 2, Fiche 3.

BELLIN, W. (1983), 'Welsh and English in Wales', in P. TRUDGILL (ed.), *Languages in the British Isles,* Cambridge University Press.

BERDAN, R. (1981), 'Black English and dialect - fair instruction, in N. MERCER (ed.), *Language in School and Community,* Edward Arnold, pp.217-36.

BEREITER, C. et al. (1966), 'An academically orientated pre-school for culturally deprived children', in F. HECHINGER (ed.), *Pre-School Education Today,* New York: Doubleday, pp.105-37.

BERNSTEIN, B. (1973), *Class, Codes and Control,* Vol. 1, Routledge & Kegan Paul.

BICKERTON, D. (1981), *Roots of Language,* Ann Arbor, Michigan: Karoma Press.

BRIDGES, D. (1979), *Education, Democracy and Discussion,* Windsor: National Foundation for Education Research.

BROOK, M. (1980), 'The Mother Tongue Issue in Britain: Cultural Diversity or Control?', *British Journal of the Sociology of Education* 1(3): 237-55.

BULLOCK, Sir A. (1975), *A Language for Life,* HMSO.

CAMPBELL-PLATT, K. (1976), 'Distribution of linguistic minorities in Britain', in G. PERREN (ed.), pp.15-30.

CARTER, T. (1971), 'Cultural content for linguistically different learners', *Elementary English* 48: 162-175.

CHESHIRE, J. (1982a), 'Dialect features and linguistic conflict in school', *Educational Review* 34, 1: 53-67.

CHESHIRE, J. (1982b). *Variation in a British Dialect: a sociolinguistic study,* Cambridge University Press.

CHOY, S. & DODD, D. (1976), 'Standard-English-speaking and non-standard Hawaiian-English-speaking children: comprehension of both dialects and teachers' evaluations', *Journal of Educational Psychology* 68: 184-93.

CLOUGH, E. & QUARMBY, J. (1979), *A Public Library Service for Ethnic Minorities in Great Britain,* Library Association (7 Ridgmount Street, London WC1E 7AE).

COHEN, A., FRIER, V. & FLORES, M. (1973), 'The Culver City Spanish Immersion Program: End of year #1 and Year #2', mimeo, Department of English, University of California at Los Angeles.

COLE, R. & WYATT, J. (1981), *Keeping in Touch,* Macmillan.

COMMISSION FOR RACIAL EQUALITY (CRE) (1980), *The EEC's Directive on the Education of Children of Migrant Workers. Its implication for the education of children from ethnic minority groups in the UK,* HMSO.

COMMISSION FOR RACIAL EQUALITY (1982), *Ethnic Minority Community Languages: a statement*, July, HMSO.

COMMONWEALTH IMMIGRANTS ADVISORY COMMITTEE (CIAC) (1964), *Second Report of the Commonwealth Immigrants Advisory Council* (Cmnd. 2266), HMSO.

COMMUNITY RELATIONS COMMISSION (CRC) (1976), *The Select Committee on Race Relations and Immigration Enquiry on the West Indian Community. Evidence on Education from the Community Relations Commission,* CRC.

COMMUNITY RELATIONS COMMISSION (CRC) (1977), *The Education of Ethnic Minority Children,* CRC.

COUNCIL OF EUROPE (1975a), Meeting of experts on curricula for children of migrant workers, 26-27 June 1975, Strasbourg.

COUNCIL OF EUROPE (1975b), Meeting of experts on the teaching of the language of the host country to children of migrant workers, 30-31 October 1975, Strasbourg.

COUNCIL OF EUROPE (1977), Council Directive on the education of the children of migrant workers (77/48b/EEC), 25 July.

CRUMP, S. (1979), 'The Language of West Indian Children and its Relevance for Schools'. Unpublished MA dissertation, University of London Institute of Education. Not available for loan.

CUMMINS, J. (1981), 'Biliteracy, language proficiency and educational programs', in J. EDWARDS (ed.) (1981), pp.131-46.

DARCY, N. (1953), 'A review of the literature on the effects of bilingualism upon the measurement of intelligence', *Journal of Genetic Psychology* 82: 21-57.

DAY, R. (1982), 'Children's attitudes towards language', in RYAN, E. & GILES, H. (1982), pp.116-31.

DERRICK, J. (1967), *English for the Children of Immigrants* (Schools Council Working Paper No. 13), HMSO.

DES (1965), Circular 7/65: 'The Education of Immigrants.'

DES (1971a), *Potential and Progress in a Second Culture,* HMSO.

DES (1971b), *The Education of Immigrants* (Education Survey 13.) HMSO.

DES (1972), *The Continuing Needs of Immigrants,* HMSO.

DES (1981), Circular 5/81, 31st July (Welsh Office Circular No. 36/81) 'Directive of the Council of Europe on the Education of the Children of Migrant Workers'.

DILLARD, J. (1978). 'Bidialectal Education: Black English and Standard English in the United States', in B. SPOLSKY & R. COOPER (eds.), *Case Studies in Bilingual Education,* Rowley, Mass: Newbury House.

DIXON, B. (1977), *Catching Them Young* (2 vols.), Pluto Press.

DOUGHTY, P., PIERCE, J. & THORNTON, G. (1971), *Language in Use,* Edward Arnold for the Schools Council.

DOWNING, J. (1978), 'Strategies of bilingual teaching', *International Review of Education* 24: 329-346.

EDWARDS, J. (1977), 'The speech of disadvantaged Dublin children', *Language Problems and Language Planning* 1: 65-72.

EDWARDS, J. (1979a), 'Judgements and confidence in reaction to disadvantaged speech', in GILES, H. & ST CLAIR, R. (eds.), *Language and Social Psychology,* Oxford: Basil Blackwell, pp.22-44.

EDWARDS, J. (1979b), *Language and Disadvantage,* Edward Arnold.

EDWARDS, J. (ed.) (1981a), *The Social Psychology of Reading,* Silver Spring, Maryland: Institute of Modern Languages Inc.

EDWARDS, J. (1981b), 'The context of bilingual education', *Journal of Multilingual and Multicultural Development* 2(11): 25-44.

EDWARDS, V. (1979), *The West Indian Language Issue in British Schools. Challenges and Responses,* Routledge & Kegan Paul.

EDWARDS, V. (1981), 'Black British English. A bibliographical essay on the language of children of West Indian origin', *Sage Race Relations Abstracts* 5(3 and 4): 1-26.

EDWARDS, V. (1982), 'Research priorities in the study of British Black English'. Paper given at the British Association of Applied Linguistics conference on Language and Ethnicity, January.

EDWARDS, V. (1983), 'Dialect speakers: fact and fantasy', *Early Child Development and care,* 9.

EDWARDS, V. (1984), 'Language policy in multicultural Britain', in J. EDWARDS (ed.), *Bilingualism, Pluralism, and Language Planning Policies,* Academic Press.

EDWARDS, V. & WELTENS, B. (in press), 'Research on non-standard dialects of

British English: progress and prospects', in W. VIERECK (ed.), *Focus on British English*, Heidelberg: Julius Groos Verlag.

ENGLES, D. (1975), *The Use of Vernacular Languages in Education*, Arlington, Va.: Center for Applied Linguistics.

EUROPEAN COMMUNITIES COMMISSION (1976), 'An education policy for the Community. Resolution of the Council and of the Ministers of Education. Meeting within the Council of 9 February 1976.' Background note published 26 March 1976.

EVANS, E. (1978), 'Welsh', in C. JAMES (ed.) (1978), pp.7-35.

FAGAN, S. (1958), 'Analysis of the Written English of some Jamaican City Children'. Unpublished MA thesis, University of London.

FATHMAN, A. (1976), 'Variables affecting the successful learning of English as a second language', *TESOL* 10(4): 433-41.

FISHMAN, J. (1976). *Bilingual Education: An International Sociological Perspective*, Rowley, Massachusetts: Newbury House.

FRENDER, R., BROWN, B. & LAMBERT, W. (1970), 'The role of speech characteristics in scholastic success', *Canadian Journal of Behavioural Science* 2: 299-306.

GANNON, P. & CZERNIEWSKA, P. (1980), *Using Linguistics. An educational focus*, Edward Arnold.

GARTON, J. (1980), 'Aspects of bilingualism in Sikh children in Slough: a pilot questionnaire', MAAL Project, Department of Linguistic Science, University of Reading.

GARVIE, E. (1982), 'English as a second language in multi-cultural education - a change of role', *Cambridge Journal of Education* 12 (2): 87-100.

GENESEE, F. (1979), 'Acquisition of reading skills in immersion programs', *Foreign Language Annals*, February.

GHUMAN, P. (1980), 'Punjabi parents and English education', *Educational Research* 22(2): 121-30.

GILES, H. & POWESLAND, P. (1975), *Speech Style and Social Evaluation*, Academic Press.

GILES, H., BOURHIS, R., TRUDGILL, P. & LEWIS, A. (1974), 'The imposed norm hypothesis: a validation', *Quarterly Journal of Speech*, 60: 405-410.

GILES, H., BOURHIS, R. & DAVIES, A. (1975), 'Prestige speech styles: the imposed norm and inherent value hypothesis', in W. McCORMACK & S. WURM (eds.), *Language in Anthropology IV: Language in Many Ways*, The Hague: Mouton.

GILES, W. (1971), 'Cultural contrasts in English-French bilingual instruction in the early grades'. Paper presented at the Conference on Child Language, Chicago.

GOLLASCH, F. (1981), *Language and Literacy: The Selected Writings of Kenneth S. Goodman*, Vol. 1: *Process, Theory, Research*, Routledge & Kegan Paul.

GOODMAN, K. & BUCK, C. (1973), 'Dialect barriers to comprehension revisited', *The Reading Teacher* 27: 6-12.

GOODMAN, K., GOODMAN, V. & FLORES, B. (1979), *Reading in The Bilingual Classroom: literacy and biliteracy,* Rosslyn, Virginia: National Clearinghouse for Bilingual Education.

GOODY, J. (1981), *Language and Dialect in the Multi-Ethnic Classroom,* ILEA.

GRANGER, R., MATTHEWS, M., QUAY, L. & VERNER, R. (1977), 'Teacher judgements of the communication effectiveness of children using different speech patterns', *Journal of Educational Psychology* 69: 793-6.

GRANT, C. (1973), 'Black studies materials do make a difference', *The Journal of Educational Research* 66: 400-4.

GRANT, G. (1974), 'The effect of text materials with relevant language, illustrations and content upon the reading achievement and reading preference (attitude) of Black primary and intermediate inner-city students.' Doctoral dissertation, University of Wisconsin, 1973. *Dissertation Abstracts International* 34, 3832A (University Microfilms No. 73-21, 156).

GRAVES, R. (1978), 'Bullock and beyond: research on the writing process', in F. DAVIS & R. PARKER (eds.), *Teaching for Literacy: Reflections on the Bullock Report,* Ward Lock.

GRUNDIN, H. (1980), 'Reading schemes in the Infant School', *Reading* 14(1): 5-13.

HADI, S. (1976), 'Some Language Issues'. Unpublished paper based on a survey undertaken as part of the Schools Council/NFER 'Education for a Multiracial Society' Project.

HALLIDAY, D. (1981), 'Mother tongue teaching – approaches and controversies'. Paper compiled by participants in a conference organised by the DES at Bedford College of Higher Education, September.

HARBER, J. (1981), 'The effect of cultural and linguistic differences on reading performance', in J. EDWARDS (ed.) (1981), pp. 173-92.

HAWKES, N. (1966), *Immigrant Children in British Schools,* Pall Mall Press for the Institute of Race Relations.

HAYNES, J. (1971), *Educational Assessment of Immigrant Pupils,* Windsor: National Foundation for Educational Research.

HEALY, M. (1981), *Your Language One, Your Language Two, Your Language Three,* Macmillan.

HEATH, C. (1980), *The Pronunciation of English in Cannock, Staffordshire. A sociolinguistic study of an urban speech community* (Publications of the Philological Society XXVIV), Oxford: Basil Blackwell.

HEBDIGE, D. (1976), 'Reggae, Rastas and Rudies', in S. HALL & T. JEFFERSON (eds.), *Resistance Through Ritual: youth sub-cultures in post-war Britain,* Hutchinson.

HERBSTEIN, D. (1980), 'I'm in need of small talk', *Sunday Times,* January 27: 12.

HMSO (1965), *Immigration from the Commonwealth,* HMSO.

HMSO (1973), *Select Committee on Race Relations and Immigration, Session 1972-3, Education,* Volume 1: *Report,* HMSO

HMSO (1977), *Select Committee on Race Relations and Immigration, Session 1976-7. The West Indian Community.* Volume 1: *Report,* HMSO.

HERNANDEZ-CHAVEZ, E., COHEN, A. & BELTRAMO, A. (1975), *El lenguaje de los Chicanos,* Arlington, Virginia: Center for Applied Linguistics.

HESTER, H., WAINWRIGHT, C. & FRASER, M. (1977), *English as a Second Language in Multi-racial Schools,* National Book League.

HIRO, D. (1973), *Black British, White British,* Penguin.

HOFFMAN, M. (1981), 'Children's reading and social values', in N. MERCER (ed.), *Language in School and Community,* pp. 192-216.

HOLLINGWORTH, B. (1977), 'Dialect in school - an historical note', *Durham and Newcastle Research Review* 8(39): 15-20.

HOUSTON, S. (1969), 'A sociolinguistic consideration of Black English children in Northern Florida', *Language* 45: 599-607.

HOYLE, S. (1978), 'Street language in an urban primary school', *Issues in Race and Education* 12.

HOYLE, S. (1982), 'Music in the classroom', *Educational Journal* IV(1): 1-7.

HUGHES, A. & TRUDGILL, P. (1979), *English Accents and Dialects. An Introduction to Social and Regional Varieties of British English,* Edward Arnold.

INNER LONDON EDUCATION AUTHORITY (ILEA) (1967), *The Education of Immigrant Pupils in Primary Schools.* Report of a Working Party of the Inspectorate and the School Psychological Service, ILEA.

INNER LONDON EDUCATION AUTHORITY (1972), *Literacy Survey: 1971 Follow-up Preliminary Report,* ILEA 203. RS567A/72 Research and Statistics Group.

INNER LONDON EDUCATION AUTHORITY (1977), *Multi-Ethnic Education.* Joint Report of the Schools Sub-committee presented to the Education Committee on 8 November.

JACKSON, L. (1974), 'The myth of elaborated and restricted code', *Higher Education Review* 6(2): 47, 49, 65.

JAMES, C. (ed.) (1978), *The Older Mother Tongues of the United Kingdom,* Centre for Information on Language Teaching and Research.

JEFFCOATE, R. (1979), *Positive Image: towards a multiracial curriculum,* Chameleon for Writers and Readers Publishing Cooperative.

JOHNSON, J. (1978), 'Ballad for You', *Race Today,* January/February.

KACHRU, B. (1978), 'Toward structuring code-mixing: an Indian perspective', *International Journal of the Sociology of Language* 16: 27-46.

KNOWLES, G. (1974), 'Scouse: the urban dialect of Liverpool'. Unpublished Ph.D. thesis, University of Leeds.

KOHL, H. (1967), *Thirty Six Children,* New York: New American Library.

KRESS, G. (1982), *Learning to Write,* Routledge & Kegan Paul.

LABOV, W. (1966), *The Social Stratification of English in New York City,* Washington D.C.: Center for Applied Linguistics.

LABOV, W. (1969), 'The logic of nonstandard English', *Georgetown Monographs on Language and Linguistics,* Vol. 22: 1-31. Reprinted in N. KEDDIE (ed.) (1973), *Tinker, Tailor . . . The Myth of Cultural Deprivation,* Penguin, pp. 21-66.

LABOV, W. & ROBINS, C. (1972), 'A note on the relation of reading failure to peer group status in urban ghettos', in W. LABOV (ed.), *Language in the Inner City,* Philadelphia: University of Pennsylvania Press, pp. 241-54.

LADD, P. & EDWARDS, V. (1982), 'British sign language and West Indian Creole', *Sign Language Studies* 35: 101-26.

LAMBERT, W., HODGSON, R., GARDNER, R. & FILLENBAUM, S. (1960), 'Evaluational reactions to spoken languages', *Journal of Abnormal and Social Psychology* 60: 44-51.

LAMBERT, W. & TUCKER, G. (1972), *Bilingual Education of Children: The St Lambert Experiment,* Rowley, Mass: Newbury House.

LANDER, S. (1979), 'Morpho-Syntactic Features in the Writing of Second Generation West Indian', MA dissertation, Dept of Engish Language and Linguistics, University of Sheffield.

LANDER, S. (1981), 'Attitudes towards non-standard grammatical features in written narrative'. Unpublished paper given at British Pychological Society Conference 1981.

LANDER, S. (undated), 'A Report on Non-standard Features found in the Written English of Ethnic Minority Schoolchildren in Sheffield', Dept of Linguistics, Sheffield University.

LEE, W. (1968), 'Thoughts on contrastive linguistics in the context of language teaching', in J. ALATIS (ed.) *Monograph Series on Languages and Linguistics 21: Contrastive Linguistics and its Pedagogical Implications,* Washington D.C.: Georgetown University Press, pp. 185-94.

LEITCH, J. (1979), 'West Indian language: the state of play', *Caribbean Teachers Association Quarterly Newsletter* 12.

LEVINE, J. (1982), 'Developing pedagogies for multilingual classes', *English in Education* 15(3): 25-33.

LINGUISTIC MINORITIES PROJECT (1983), *Linguistic Minorities in England,* Routledge & Kegan Paul.

LITTLE, A. & WILLEY, R. (1981), *Multi-ethnic Education: The Way Forward,* Schools Council Pamphlet No. 18, Schools Council.

MACAULAY, R. with the assistance of TREVELYAN, G. (1977), *Language, Social Class and Education: A Glasgow Study,* Edinburgh University Press.

McLEOD, A. (1982a), 'Why don't we study writing?' Paper given at 'Languages and Ethnicity', seminar jointly organized by the Linguistic Minorities Project and the British Association of Applied Linguistics, London.

McLEOD, A. (1982b), 'Writing. Dialect and linguistic awareness', in *Talk Workshop Group* (1982), pp.423-41.

MacNAMARA, J. (1974), 'What can we expect of a bilingual programme?' *Working Papers in Bilingualism* 4.

McNEIL, F. & MERCER, N. (1982), *The Primary Language Project: Here I Am; Language Around Us; Talking and Feeling.* A.& C. Black.

MERCER, L. (1981), 'Ethnicity and the supplementary school', in N. MERCER (ed.), *Language in School and Community,* Edward Arnold, pp.147-60.

MERCER, N. (1981), *Language in School and Community,* Edward Arnold.

MERCER, N., MERCER, E. & MEARS, R. (1979), 'Linguistic and cultural affiliation amongst young Asian people in Leicester', in H. GILES & B. SAINT-JACQUES (eds.), *Language and Ethnic Relations,* Oxford: Pergamon Press, pp. 15-26.

MILROY, L. (1980), *Language and Social Networks,* Oxford: Basil Blackwell.

MITTINS, W. et al. (1970), *Attitudes to English Usage: an enquiry by the University of Newcastle upon Tyne Institute of Education Research Group,* Oxford University Press.

MOON, C. & RABAN, B. (1980), *A Question of Reading* (Revised Edition), Macmillan.

NATIONAL ASSOCIATION FOR MULTIRACIAL EDUCATION (NAME) (undated), *Policy Statement: Mother Tongue and Minority Community Languages in Education,* Mickleover, Derby: NAME.

NATIONAL ASSOCIATION FOR THE TEACHING OF ENGLISH (NATE) (undated), *The Teaching of English in Multicultural Britain.* A discussion document prepared by a working party of NATE.

NATIONAL ASSOCIATION OF SCHOOLMASTERS (NAS) (1969), *Education and the Immigrants,* Hemel Hempstead, Herts: Educare.

NATIONAL FOUNDATION FOR EDUCATIONAL RESEARCH (NFER) (1973), *Tests for Proficiency in English,* Ginn.

NEALE, M. (1958), *The Analysis of Reading Ability,* Macmillan.

NEWBOLT, H. (1921), *The Teaching of English in England,* HMSO.

NEWBROOK, M. (1921), 'Sociolinguistic reflexes of dialect intereference in West Wirral'. Unpublished Ph.D. thesis, University of Reading.

NEWBY, M. (1981), *Making Language* (Books 1, 2, 3), Oxford University Press.

NEWSOM, J. (1963), *Half Our Future,* HMSO.

OPIE, I. & OPIE, P. (1977), *The Lore and Language of Schoolchildren,* St Albans: Paladin.

ORTON, H. et al. (1962-71), *Survey of English Dialects: Basic Material,* Leeds: E. J. Arnold.

ÖSTERBERG, T. (1961), *Bilingualism and the First School Language,* Umea: Västerbottens Tryckeri.

PALMER, P. (1981), 'An Investigation into the Language Use of Children of Jamaican Origin in Manchester'. MAAL project, Dept of Linguistic Science, University of Reading.

PEAL, E. & LAMBERT, W. (1962), 'The relation of bilingualism to intelligence', *Psychological Monographs* 76: 546.

PERREN, G. (1976), *Bilingualism and British Education: the Dimensions of Diversity* (CILT Reports and Papers 14), Centre for Information on Language Teaching and Research.

PIDGEON, W. (1970), *Teacher Expectation and Pupil Performance,* Windsor: National Foundation for Educational Research.

PLOWDEN, B. (1967), *Children and their Primary Schools,* HMSO.

POWER, J. (1967), *Immigrants in School. A survey of administrative policies,* Councils and Education Press Ltd.

RABAN, B. (1982), 'Influences on children's writing 5-9 years'. Paper presented at the United Kingdom Reading Association Conference, Newcastle.

RAMOS, M. ANGUILAR, J. & SIBAYAN, B. (1967), *The Determination and Implementation of Language Policy,* Quezon City: Phoenix Press.

RAMPTON, A. (1981), *West Indian Children in Our Schools* (Interim report of the Committee of Inquiry into the Education of Children from Ethnic Minority Groups), HMSO.

RAMPTON, M. B. (1981), 'The English of UK Ethnic Minority School Children of South Asian Extraction'. M.A. dissertation, University of London Institute of Education.

REES, O., FITZPATRICK, B. et al. (1981), *Mother Tongue and English Teaching Project* (Summary of the Report, volumes I and II), Bradford College.

RICHARDSON, R. (1982), 'Talking about equality: the use and importance of discussion in multi-cultural education', *Cambridge Journal of Education* 12(2): 101-114.

RICHMOND, J. (1978), 'Jennifer and Brixton Blues', *New Approaches to Multiracial Education* 6(3).

RICHMOND, J. (1979), 'Dialect features in mainstream school writing', *New Approaches to Multiracial Education* 8(1): 9-15.

RICHMOND, J. (1982), *The Resources of Classroom Language,* Edward Arnold.

RICHMOND, J. & McLEOD, A. (1981), 'Craft and art in children's writing', *English Magazine* No. 6: 4-10.

RICHMOND. J. & SAVVA, H. (1983), *Investigating our Language,* Edward Arnold.

RILEY, K. (1982), 'Policing the police, teaching the teachers: Scarman, Rampton and MPs read the riot lessons', *Multiracial Education* 10(2): 3-10.

ROSE, E. et al. (1969), *Colour and Citizenship. A report on British race relations,* Published for the Institute of Race Relations by Oxford University Press.

ROSEN, C. & ROSEN, H. (1973), *The Language of Primary School Children,* Penguin.

ROSEN, H. & BURGESS, T. (1980), *Language and Dialects of London School Children,* Ward Lock Educational.

ROSEN, M. (1982), 'Three Papers: Writers in inner city residence; In their own voice; Our culture – a definition by description of its parts', in *Talk Workshop* (1982), pp.378-91.

RYAN, E. & GILES, H. (1982), *Attitudes towards Language Variation: Social and Applied Contexts,* Edward Arnold.

RYAN, W. (1976), *Blaming the Victim,* New York: Vintage Books.

SAIFULLAH KHAN, V. (1976), 'Provision by minorities for language maintenance', in G. PERREN (ed.) (1976), pp.31-47.

SAIFULLAH KHAN, V. (1980), 'The mother-tongue of linguistic minorities in multicultural England', *Journal of Multilingual and Multicultural Development* 1(i): 71-88.

SAVILLE-TROIKE, M. (1982), *The Ethnography of Communication,* Oxford: Basil Blackwell.

SELIGMAN, C., TUCKER, G. & LAMBERT, W. (1972), 'The effects of speech style and other attributes on teachers' attitudes towards pupils', *Language in Society* 1: 131-42.

SELINKER, L. (1972), 'Interlanguage' (IRAL no. 10(3): 219-31) reprinted in J. RICHARDS (ed.), *Error Analysis*, Longman, pp.31-54.

SEWAK, H. (1982), 'Mother tongue: the importance of Asian languages in Britain', in *Talking and Telling* (Yearbook of the Language Support Services in Berkshire), pp.67-9. Available from the English Language Centre, Lydford Road, Reading.

SHAUGHNESSY, M. (1977), *Errors and Expectations. A guide for the teacher of basic writing,* New York: Oxford University Press.

SHUY, R. (1977), 'Implications of recent sociolinguistic research for the problems of migrant worker children' in M. DE GRÈVE & E. ROSSEEL (eds.) *Problèmes linguistiques des enfants de travailleurs migrants,* Brussels: AIMAV/Didier, pp.187-210.

SINCLAIR, J. &COULTHARD, M. (1975), *Towards an Analysis of Discourse: The English used by teachers and pupils,* Oxford University Press.

SMITH, F. (1978), *Reading,* Cambridge University Press.

SMITH, F. (1982), *Writing and the writer,* Heinemann Educational.

SNOW, R. (1969), 'Review of *Pygmalion in the Classroom* by Rosenthal and Jakobson', *Contemporary Psychology* 41:197-9.

SOUTHGATE, V., ARNOLD, H. & JOHNSON, S. (1981), *Extending Beginning Reading,* Heinemann Educational for the Schools Council.

SPENS, W. (1969)., *Learning Discussion Skills Through Games,* New York: Citation Press.

STANFORD, G. (1969), *Learning Discussion Skills Through Games*, New York: Citation Press.

STONE, M. (1981), *The Education of the Black Child in Britain*, Fontana.

STUBBS, M. (1976), *Language, Schools and Classrooms,* Methuen.

STUDDERT, J. & WILES, S. (1982), 'Children's writing in the multilingual classroom', *Centre for Urban Educational Studies Occasional Papers*, Spring.

SUTCLIFFE, D. (1978), 'The Language of First and Second Generation West Indian Children in Bedfordshire'. M.Ed. thesis, University of Leicester.

SUTCLIFFE, D. (1982), *British Black English,* Oxford: Basil Blackwell.

TALK WORKSHOP GROUP (1982), *Becoming Our Own Experts. The Vauxhall Papers.* Available from ILEA English Centre, Sutherland Street, London SW1.

TALBERT, C. (1969), 'Sociolinguistic analysis of teachers and pupils'. Paper delivered at the 1969 Annual Meeting of the American Anthropological Association.

THOMAS, R. (1969), 'Vindication and Infringement: Towards an ethnographic analysis of classroom interaction'. Unpublished M.A. dissertation, University of London Institute of Education. Not available on loan.

THORNDIKE, R. (1968), 'Review of Rosenthal and Jacobson, *Pygmalion in the Classroom',* American Educational Research Journal* 5(4). 708-11.

TIZARD, B., CARMICHAEL H., HUGHES, M. & PINKERTON, G. (1980), 'Four year olds talking to mothers and teachers', in L. HERSOV & M. BERGER (eds.), *Language and Language Disorders in Childhood,* Oxford: Pergamon Press, pp.49-76.

TODD, L. (1974), *Pidgins and Creoles,* Routledge & Kegan Paul.

TOMLIN, C. (1981), 'The Extent to which West Indian Linguistic Differences Hinder or Enhance Learning'. Unpublished dissertation, Dudley College of Education.

TOSI, A. (1979), 'Mother tongue teaching for children of migrants', *Language Teaching and Linguistics Abstracts* 213-31.

TOWNSEND, H. (1971), *Immigrants in England: the LEA response,* Windsor: National Foundation for Educational Research.

TOWNSEND, H. & BRITTAN, E. (1972), *Organisation in Multi-racial Schools,* Windsor: National Foundation for Educational Research.

TOWNSEND, H. & BRITTAN, E. (1973), *Multiracial Education: Need and Innovation,* Methuen for the Schools Council.

TROIKE, R. (1978), 'Research evidence for the effectiveness of bilingual education', *NABE Journal,* 3: 13-24.

TRUDGILL, P. (1974), *The Social Differentiation of English in Norwich,* Cambridge University Press.

TRUDGILL, P. (1975), *Accent, Dialect and the School,* Edward Arnold.

TRUDGILL, P. (ed.) (1978), *Sociolinguistic Patterns in British English,* Edward Arnold.

TRUDGILL, P. (1979a), 'Standard and non-standard dialects of English in the United Kingdom: problems and policies', *International Journal of the Sociology of Language* 21: 9-24.

TRUDGILL, P. (1979b), *Sociolinguistics: An Introduction,* Penguin.

TRUDGILL, P. (1982), *On Dialect: Social and geographical perspectives,* Oxford: Basil Blackwell.

TRUDGILL, P. (ed.) (1983), *Language in the British Isles,* Cambridge University Press.

TSOW, M. (forthcoming), 'National Survey of LEAs on Mother Tongue Teaching, 1981-2', *Educational Research.*

TWITCHIN, J. & DEMUTH, C. (1981), *Multicultural Education,* BBC.

URE, J. (1974), 'Code-switching and "mixed speech" in the register systems of developing languages', in A. VERDOOT (ed.), *Proceedings of the 3rd International Congress of Applied Linguistics.* Vol. 11: *Applied Sociolinguistics,* Heidelberg: Julius Groos Verlag.

VENEZKY, W. (1981), 'Non-standard language and reading - ten years later', in J. EDWARDS (ed.) (1981), pp.193-206.

VERMA, G. & BAGLEY, C. (1975), *Race and Education Across Cultures,* Heinemann.

VULLIAMY, G. & LEE, E. (eds.) (1980), *Pop Music in Schools,* Cambridge University Press.

WEIGHTMAN, J. (1982), 'Creating a ghetto mentality?' *Times Educational Supplement,* April 16th: 20.

WEINREICH, U. (1968), *Languages in Contact,* The Hague: Mouton.

WHITELEY, W. H. (ed.) (1971), *Language Use and Social Change. Problems of multilingualism with special reference to Eastern Africa,* Oxford University Press for the International African Institute.

WIGHT, J. (1969), 'Teaching English to West Indian children', *English for Immigrants* 2(2).

WIGHT, J. (1970), 'Language, deprivation and remedial teaching techniques', in ATEPO (1970).

WIGHT, J. (1976), 'How much interference?' *Times Educational Supplement,* 14 May.

WIGHT, J., HUNT, P., SAPARA, S. & SINCLAIR, H. (1978a), *Share-a-Story,* Edinburgh: Holmes McDougall in collaboration with ILEA Learning Materials Service.

WIGHT, J., HUNT, P., SAPARA, S. & SINCLAIR, H. (1978b), *Make-a-Story,* ILEA Learning Materials Service.

WIGHT, J. & NORRIS, R. (1970), *Teaching English to West Indian Children. The research stage of the project.* (Schools Council Working Paper 29), Evans/Methuen.

WILDING, J. (1982), *Ethnic Minority Languages in the Classroom? A survey of Asian parents in Leicester,* Leicester: Leicester Council for Community Relations and Leicester City Council.

WILES, S. (1981), 'Language issues in the multicultural classroom', in N. MERCER (ed.), *Language in School and Community,* Edward Arnold, pp.51-76.

WILLIAMS, F. et al. (1976), *Explorations of the Linguistic Attitudes of Teachers,* Rowley, Mass: Newbury House.

WOOD, D., McMAHON, L. & CRANSTOUN, Y. (1980), *Working with Under Fives,* Grant McIntyre.

WRIGHT, J. (1978), *Bilingualism in Education* (CUES Occasional Paper No. 1.), Centre for Urban Educational Studies.

Index